Moulinex Regal

Getting More From Your Food Processor

With tips for successful use of your processor, menu suggestions, and more than 200 recipes developed specifically for preparation in the food processor.

Marilyn Kostick

Dorison House Publishers/Boston

The Author

Marilyn Kostick has a BA degree in home economics from the University of Iowa and an MA degree in education from Long Island University. She has worked as a hospital dietician, nutritionist, teacher and cookbook editor. In recent years she has traveled extensively and enjoys trying foreign cuisines. She ranks the food processor as her number one favorite kitchen appliance.

Acknowledgements

Thanks to Pat Palmer of Dorison House Publishers for the breads and rolls she baked and shared with all of us.

Thanks to Jerome Rubin, cookbook author, for his assistance in testing recipes.

Thanks to all our friends who tasted and critiqued with enthusiasm.

Thanks to Adeline Halfmann of Regal Ware, Inc. for her cooperation in making this book possible.

Copyright © 1984 by Dorison House Publishers, Inc.
Published by Dorison House Publishers, Inc.
824 Park Square Building, Boston, MA 02116

ISBN: 0-916752-63-1
Library of Congress Catalog Number: 84-070240
Manufactured in the United States of America

NOTE:
If you have any questions or problems about any of the recipes in this cookbook, please write or call Dorison House Publishers and ask for Marilyn or Pat. We'll be happy to try to help.

Design: Myra Lee Conway/Design
Boston, MA

Contents

Introduction

Your food processor brings you a whole new world of culinary adventure. Once you have become familiar with it, you'll find it can perform food preparation tasks with phenomenal speed and efficiency.

What does it do? It combines the functions of several appliances as it mixes batters for cakes and cookies, blends spreads, dips and salad dressings, grinds, purées, slices, chops and shreds raw and cooked food, crumbs breads, cookies and crackers, and kneads doughs for bread. With the new Beater Accessory it can also whip cream and egg whites. It works fast, takes up a minimum of kitchen counter space, is attractively designed, and can be easily cleaned. No wonder cooks everywhere are thrilled to have this helper in their kitchens.

This cookbook was written to help maximize your use of the processor. We have developed and tested more than 200 recipes; some of them would have been practically impossible for anyone but a skilled chef before the introduction of the food processor. The directions are detailed, and in the beginning, we suggest you follow them carefully. As you gain experience, of course, you will want to let your imagination soar, and make your own creations. Mainly, we hope you enjoy getting more from your food processor.

Getting to Know La Machine™

FOOD PUSHER. The Food Pusher fits inside the Feed Tube to guide food onto the Discs and to prevent liquid from splashing out. It can be used as a measuring cup as it is marked in ounces and milliliters. Never use your fingers when machine is in operation.

COVER WITH FEED TUBE. Ingredients are fed through the Feed Tube into the processor. Solid foods are stacked to be sliced or shredded, and eased down the Feed Tube with firm gentle pressure of the Food Pusher. Liquid ingredients, and such dry ingredients as flour and sugar can be poured directly down the Feed Tube while the processor is running.

The Cover has an interlock system that keeps the processor from operating unless it is locked properly in place.

CUTTING/CHOPPING BLADE. The most frequently used of the accessories, the Blade fits onto the center motor shaft in the Bowl. It is used to chop, mix, blend, purée and knead bread, rolls and pie doughs. Needless to say, this is a sharp instrument and should be handled carefully.

REVERSIBLE SLICING/ SHREDDING DISC. The Disc has a serrated slicing blade on one side and a shredding blade on opposite side. Slices will be thicker as you increase the pressure on the Food Pusher, but heavy pressure on the shredder will not speed up the process and may bend or dull the Disc. The Disc must be very sharp to do a good job, so, of course, you should watch your hands.

DISC ADAPTER. The adapter is inserted into the Disc and positioned on the motor shaft in the center of Bowl when it is on motor base.

BOWL. This extra-large 72-ounce Bowl has special side locking tabs for its interlock system which prevents the processor from being turned on until it is in place.

MOTOR POWER BASE with ON-OFF PULSE SWITCH. The powerful motor is under your control. Press down for as long or as short a period of time as you need. This "spurt on and off" action is especially helpful when starting to chop large nuts or chunks of meat, and to prevent overprocessing.

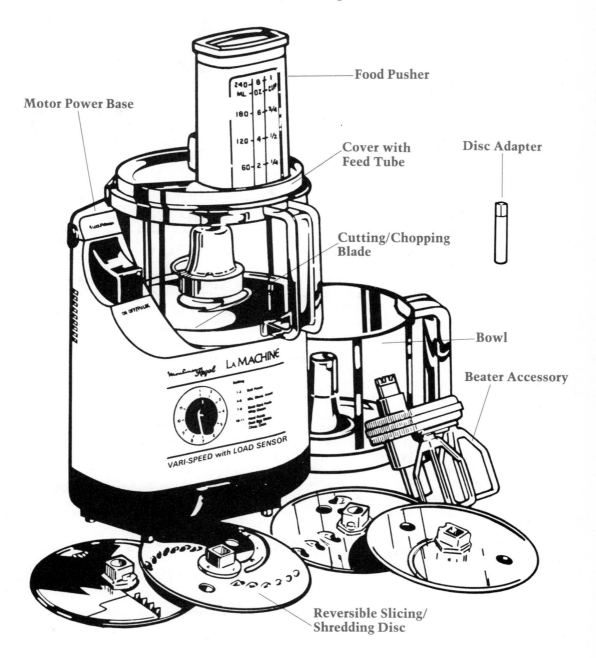

Motor Power Base

Food Pusher

Cover with Feed Tube

Disc Adapter

Cutting/Chopping Blade

Bowl

Beater Accessory

Reversible Slicing/ Shredding Disc

Getting the Best Results

- Check frequently when you begin to process a food to see how finely it is chopped. Remember, you can always chop or mix a little longer, but there is no way to reverse the process.

- Always leave Blade or Disc in Bowl when lifting it from the base; this prevents liquid or food from spilling down the central spindle. When emptying liquids from the Bowl, hold the Blade in place while pouring by pressing on the plastic handle, then remove the Blade before scraping the Bowl with a rubber spatula.

- If there is a build up of shredded or sliced food on one side of the Bowl, remove Cover and Disc and redistribute or remove food and resume processing. Be sure to stop the processor while you arrange food in the Feed Tube to reduce the chance of accident.

- Do not overload the processor. It is better to process several batches rather than one large one. At any one time, don't process more than 3½ cups of thin liquid or 6 cups of thick mixtures like dough. You can chop 1 pound of trimmed meat or mix about 3 cups of flour. Allow the machine to cool intermittently if processing very large quantities of food.

- When foods are too large to fit into the top of Feed Tube, try inserting them from the bottom.

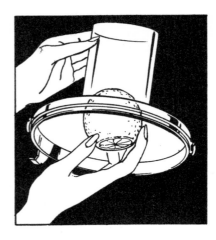

Food Processor Limitations

Don't Try to:

- Grind coffee beans or wheat or rye kernels for flour.
- Slice very soft cheese at room temperature.
- Slice or shred dried fruits (unless they have been soaked until soft).
- Grate or chop ice.
- Whip cream or egg whites to stiff peaks with the Blade. The Beater Accessory, however, does a fine job with 2 or more eggs.
- Churn butter.
- Slice, shred or mash cooked potatoes. (It makes them gluey.)
- Beat fudge so long that it loses its shine.

Food Processing Techniques

BREADS, CRACKERS and COOKIES

To make crumbs:
1. Place Blade in Bowl; add about 3 cups or less of food.

2. Pulse on and off for the first minute, then let run continuously until desired consistency is obtained.

To Bake Better Breads:

Read through the recipe.

- Organize and assemble your ingredients. Have your eggs cracked, liquids measured, nuts chopped, pans greased and oven preheated. This is especially helpful when preparing quick breads and muffins. Processing takes seconds if you're prepared!

- Remember environmental conditions affect yeast breads. It may be necessary to add a little more flour or liquid than what's called for in the recipe.

- If your processor sounds strained during the kneading, **immediately** turn it off. Remove the dough and proceed with the recipe, kneading it on the counter, if necessary.

- The recipes in this chapter were tested with all-purpose white flour. However, you may substitute whole wheat flour for ⅓ to ½ of the total flour. The resulting bread will be heavier.

- Almost all breads and rolls should be removed from pans immediately and cooled on wire racks. Some quick breads and muffins need to rest in their pans for a few minutes.

- Be flexible and imaginative. Substitute currants for raisins, cream for milk, dates for nuts and so forth.

- Before trying your own bread recipes in the food processor, remember: the recipe should contain **no more than 3 cups of flour.** Determine your procedure by following directions in these recipes. Generally, we found breads come out best when liquids were added to dry ingredients.

CHEESES

Harder cheeses like Parmesan and Romano should be at room temperature. If the cheese is too hard to cut with a knife, do not try to process it.

Soft cheeses should be chilled before slicing or shredding.

1. Cut cheese to fit Feed Tube. Place Disc, shred side up, in Bowl. Pack cheese into Feed Tube with flat edge down; shred and remove Disc and cheese.
2. Place Blade in Bowl; process until it reaches the degree of fineness you desire.

COCONUT

To prepare fresh grated coconut:

1. Use a hammer to break the coconut; pour out the milk, and place the pieces in a warm oven for about 10 minutes or microwave for 5 minutes. The hard shell will be easy to remove. Use a sharp knife to peel off the dark skin.
2. Place Disc, shred side up, in Bowl; shred coconut.
3. Place Blade in Bowl; process to finely grate coconut.

Makes: 3 cups from 1 medium (4-inches in diameter) coconut.

NOTE: If you wish to freeze grated coconut, reserve coconut milk. Pack cocnut in containers with coconut milk. Leave top room and seal.

7

FRUIT and VEGETABLES

To grate citrus rind:
1. Cut rind from fruit. Do not include the white part or zest because it is bitter.
2. Place Blade in Bowl; add rind and sugar from the recipe and process until finely grated.

To slice:
1. Wedge thin foods like carrots and celery tightly and vertically into Feed Tube in upright position. If they are long, cut into lengths just shorter than the length of Feed Tube, or position food sideways for longer shreds or slices.

   To slice one item, place in right side of Feed Tube. Hold in place with Food Pusher.

   For more even slicing, cut a thin slice off the end of food; place in Feed Tube with flat side toward cutting edge of Disc.
2. Slice using firm pressure.

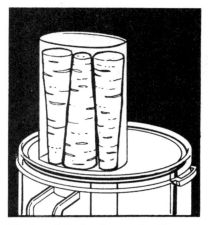

Wedge thin foods vertically; or, if they are long, position them sideways.

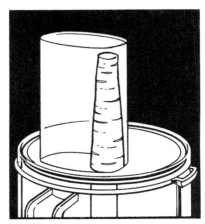

To slice one item.

To purée:
1. Pare foods before cooking for a smooth purée.
2. Place Blade in Bowl; add ½ cup liquid and 2 cups cooked food. Process until smooth, about 10 to 15 seconds. Scrape down sides as necessary.

Use vegetable purée for thickening soup and sauces, or serve it as a side dish.

To Julienne-cut vegetables.

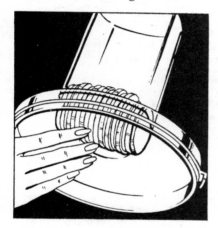

To make julienne-cut vegetables:
1. Place Disc, slice side up, in Feed Tube; slice foods.
2. Reassemble slices and fit tightly into bottom of Feed Tube with cut edges at right angles to cover.
3. Replace Disc, slice side up; slice again. This cross cutting forms small matchstick shapes.

MEAT or FISH

To grind:
1. Cut meat or fish, cooked or uncooked, into 1-inch cubes; use pulse control to start until pieces are smaller. Stir, if necessary, to distribute large pieces.
2. Continue processing until the meat is the desired texture, about 7 to 15 seconds.

To slice:
1. Cut thick pieces of meat to fit Feed Tube, trim and bone. Wrap and place in the freezer until firm but not frozen.
2. Slice using firm pressure on the Food Pusher.

NUTS

Nuts must be shelled.

To chop nuts and make nut butters:
1. Place Blade in Bowl; add 1 to 2 cups nuts; process for 4 minutes for smooth nut butter. Scrape down if necessary after 2 minutes. The longer the processing, the finer the texture.
2. For chunky nut butter add about ¼ cup nuts at end of processing; pulse on and off to chop coarsely.

The oils released during the processing cause a paste to form, so dry roasted peanuts will not work for peanut butter.

Food Processing Equivalents

This chart tells you approximately how much whole food you should chop, slice or shred to obtain the amount in cups you need in your recipe.

WHOLE FOOD	PROCESS	YIELD
Apple, 1 medium	Coarsely chopped Thinly sliced	1 cup ½ to ¾ cup
Avocado, 1 medium	Puréed Sliced	¾ to 1 cup 1½ to 2 cups
Banana, 1 medium (5 to 6-ounces)	Puréed Sliced	⅔ cup 1 cup
Beets, 3 medium cooked, (2-ounces each)	Puréed Sliced	⅔ cup 2 cups
Bread, 2 slices (with crusts)	Crumbed	1 cup
Cabbage, ½ large head	Coarsely chopped Sliced or Shredded	3 cups 4½ cups
Carrots, 1 medium	Puréed (cooked) Sliced or Shredded	¼ cup ½ cup
Celery, 2 medium ribs	Chopped or sliced	½ to ¾ cup

Cheeses:
  Cheddar, ½ pound
  Gruyere, ½ pound
  Parmesan, ½ pound
  Swiss, ½ pound
	
	Shredded
	Shredded
	Finely Grated
	Sliced
		
		2 cups
		2 cups
		1¾ cups
		24 slices

Chicken, ½ pound cooked	Chopped	1 cup
Coconut, 1 medium (5-inch diameter)	Finely Chopped	3 cups

Cookies:
  Chocolate Wafers (24)
  Ginger Snaps (17)
  Vanilla Wafers (33)
	
	Crumbed
	Crumbed
	Crumbed
		
		1¼ cup
		1 cup
		1¼ cup

Crackers:
  Grahams, 16 squares
  Saltines, 28 squares
  Zweibacks, 8 slices
	
	Crumbed
	Crumbed
	Crumbed
		
		1¼ cups
		1 cup
		1 cup

Cranberries, (12-ounces) raw, whole	Coarsely Chopped	1 cup
Cucumbers, 1 medium (6 inches in length)	Coarsely Chopped Sliced	1 cup 1¼ cups
Eggs, 1 hard-cooked	Chopped	½ cup

WHOLE FOOD	PROCESS	YIELD
Green pepper, 1 medium	Chopped or Sliced	¾ to 1 cup
Lemon, rind of 1 medium	Finely Grated	3 teaspoons
Meat, ½ pound raw or cooked	Chopped Sliced	1 cup 1½ cups
Mushrooms, 6 large, Fresh	Chopped Sliced	1 cup 1¼ cups
Nuts: (1 cup) Almonds, Pecans Walnuts Peanuts	Chopped fine Puréed to nut butter	1 cup 1 cup
Olives, 5 large, Stuffed	Chopped or Sliced	⅓ cup
Onions, yellow, 1 medium	Chopped or Sliced Minced	½ cup ⅓ cup
Orange rind, of 1 medium	Minced	6 to 8 teaspoons
Parsley, Watercress Fresh Herbs, 1 cup loosely packed leaves	Chopped Minced	½ cup ⅓ cup
Peppers, 1 medium	Chopped Sliced	1 cup 1¼ cups
Scallions, 2 medium	Chopped	2 tablespoons
Pickles, 4 large	Coarsely Chopped Sliced	1 cup 1¼ cups
Potatoes, Sweet or White, 1 medium	Chopped or Sliced	¾ cup
Squash: 1 medium Acorn, Butternut Summer, Zucchini	Coarsely Chopped Sliced Shredded	1¼ cups 1½ cups 1 cup
Tomatoes, 1 medium	Coarsely Chopped	1 cup
Turnips, 1 medium	Coarsely Chopped Puréed, cooked	⅔ cup ⅓ cup

Crumb Crusts

CHOCOLATE:

24 thin cocolate wafers (2-inches in diameter)
2 tablespoons sugar
⅓ cup butter or margarine, melted

VANILLA OR GINGERSNAP:

36 vanilla wafers or gingersnaps
1 tablespoon light brown sugar
Pinch of nutmeg or mace (optional)
⅓ cup butter or margarine, melted

LEMON:

36 lemon wafers
1 tablespoon light brown sugar
1 (2-inch) strip lemon rind
⅓ cup butter or margarine, melted

GRAHAM CRACKER:

24 (2⅜-inch square) crackers
⅓ cup sugar
⅓ cup butter or margarine, melted
Pinch nutmeg (optional)
Pinch cinnamon (optional)

1. Place Blade in Bowl. Process the wafers until they are fine crumbs. (If lemon rind is to be grated, add it to the wafers.)
2. Empty the crumbs into a mixing bowl. Add butter, sugar and seasonings; process to blend. Using a spoon, press mixture firmly and evenly against bottom and sides of a 9-inch pie pan or springform pan.
3. Bake in a preheated 350° F. oven for 10 minutes. Cool before filling. If desired, save 2 tablespoons crumbs to sprinkle on top of the pie.

Makes 1 (9-inch) pie shell.

Nut Crumb Crusts

½ cup nuts
24 vanilla wafers, gingersnaps or lemon wafers

or
18 thin chocolate wafers (2-inches in diameter)

1. Place Blade in Bowl. Process the nuts and wafers until they are fine crumbs.
2. Empty into a mixing bowl, add butter, and mix with a fork until well blended. Using a spoon, press mixture firmly and evenly against bottom and sides of a 9-inch pie pan or springform pan.
3. Bake in a preheated 350° F. oven for 10 minutes. Cool before filling.

Makes 1 (9-inch) pie shell.

Processor Pie Crust

2 cups flour
½ teaspoon salt

**⅔ cup shortening, chilled
    and cut in small pieces**
¼ cup ice water

1. Place Blade in Bowl. Add salt and shortening. Process until mixture is finely crumbled, about like cornmeal. With machine running, add water through the Feed Tube. Process just until ball forms on the blade.
2. Divide the dough in half, and wrap in waxed paper; chill for 20 to 30 minutes.
3. Roll pastry into a 12-inch circle; lift it into the pie pan. Trim excess pastry so that it is about an inch larger than the pan all around. Flute or crimp the edge and prick bottom with tines of a fork.
4. Bake in a preheated 425° F. oven 10 to 12 minutes.

Makes 2 (9-inch) pie shells or 1 (9-inch) double crust pie.

Cream Cheese Pastry

**2 (3-ounce) packages cream
    cheese, softened**
1 cup butter or margarine

2 cups flour
½ teaspoon salt

1. Place Blade in Bowl; add cream cheese and butter, processing until well blended. Add flour and salt; process until mixture forms a ball on the blade; chill.
2. Divide dough in half. On a lightly floured surface, roll out each half to a 12-inch circle. Place in 2 (9-inch) pie plates. Trim and flute edges; prick bottom and sides with a fork.
3. Bake in a preheated 450° F. oven for 12 to 15 minutes or until golden brown.

Makes 2 (9-inch) pastry shells.

VARIATIONS:

For tart shells: divide dough into 12 balls. Roll out each to a 6-inch circle. Place in 4-inch tart pans. Trim and flute edges; prick bottom and sides with a fork. Bake in a preheated 450° F. oven 8 to 10 minutes or until golden brown.

For filled pastries: divide dough in half; roll out each half to a 10-inch square. Cut into 2-inch squares.

Puff Pastry (Pâté à Chou)

As an hors d'oeuvre, this French pastry holds fish or chicken filling. For dessert, a cream filling or ice cream, topped with hot chocolate sauce or other sauce is superb.

1 cup water	**1 cup flour**
⅛ teaspoon salt	**4 eggs**
½ cup unsalted butter or margarine	

1. Bring water, salt and butter to a full boil in a large saucepan.
2. Place Blade in Bowl; add flour. With processor running, slowly add boiling water through the Feed Tube; process for half a minute until well mixed. Add eggs one at a time through the Feed Tube. Mix well between each addition. Scrape mixture from sides of bowl. After adding all the eggs, the dough should hold its shape when dropped from a spoon onto ungreased baking sheets.
3. Bake in a preheated 425° F. oven for 30 minutes or until lightly browned and crisp. Cool.
4. Split cooled cream puffs and fill.

Makes 2 dozen small puffs.

Sweet Pastry (Paté Sablée)

A delicate French pastry for open-faced fruit tarts or pies.

1¾ cups flour	**½ cup frozen butter, cut in**
3 tablespoons sugar	**½-inch pieces**
¼ teaspoon salt	**1 egg yolk**
	4 to 5 tablespoons ice water

1. Place Blade in Bowl; add flour, sugar and salt. Pulse on and off to blend. Place pieces of butter over the dry ingredients; process until the mixture is finely crumbed.
2. Drop the egg yolk through the Feed Tube; process to blend. With processor running, add the ice water through the Feed Tube. As soon as the mixture forms a ball on the blade, stop the processing.
3. Knead the dough on a lightly floured board, for about 1 minute; wrap and chill an hour or two before rolling.
4. On a lightly floured board, roll the pastry into a 15-inch circle. Lift onto the flan ring and press the pastry against the bottom and edges. Roll the overhang around the rim and flute or crimp it.
5. Cover pastry, greased-side down, with foil or waxed paper, and fill the center with dried peas, beans or rice.
6. Bake in a 400° F. oven for 10 minutes; remove the filled liner and prick the bottom and sides of the crust. Bake another 3 minutes, or until it begins to brown. Brush the pastry lightly with beaten egg white. Let pastry cool before adding the filling.

Makes pastry for 1 (12-inch) tart.

Aioli Sauce (Garlic Mayonnaise)

Serve with fish fillets.

4 garlic cloves
3 large egg yolks
2½ cups olive oil

½ teaspoon salt
1 tablespoon lemon juice

1. Place Blade in Bowl; process garlic and egg yolks for 2 to 3 seconds, until blended.
2. With the processor running, slowly pour in the olive oil, in a thin trickle at first until the mayonnaise starts to thicken, then faster. When thick, add salt and lemon juice.

Makes 2½ cups.

Uncooked Fresh Applesauce

Ascorbic acid will prevent darkening of the applesauce. It is sold in freezer departments of supermarkets and in some drug stores.

**12 medium tart apples, peeled,
cored and quartered**
**¼ cup ascorbic acid or
lemon juice**

1 cup sugar
1 teaspoon cinnamon
½ teaspoon nutmeg

1. Sprinkle ascorbic acid over prepared apples; toss to cover all sides.
2. Place Blade in Bowl; add apple quarters, 8 at a time; purée and empty into a bowl. Repeat procedure until all apples are puréed.
3. Stir in spices.

Makes 6 cups.

Aurore Sauce

Serve over chicken or fish mousse.

1 medium onion, quartered
3 shallots
5 tablespoons butter or margarine
4 tomatoes, quartered
½ teaspoon thyme
1 bay leaf

½ teaspoon tarragon
Salt and pepper
1½ tablespoons flour
1 cup chicken broth
½ cup heavy cream

1. Place Blade in Bowl; chop onion and shallots. Sauté in 2 tablespoons of the butter.
2. Chop tomatoes finely and add to onion and shallots. Add seasonings. Cook, stirring frequently, about 10 minutes.
3. In a separate saucepan, melt 3 tablespoons of the butter, and stir in flour. Add chicken broth, simmer, stirring occasionally, about 10 minutes.
4. Combine with tomato mixture. Stir in cream.

Makes 2¼ cups.

Bernaise Sauce

Serve with fish.

1 scallion, cut in 1-inch pieces
2 teaspoons lemon juice
¼ cup dry white wine
½ teaspoon tarragon
¼ teaspoon chervil
3 egg yolks
⅛ teaspoon cayenne pepper
½ cup butter or margarine, melted

1. Place Blade in Bowl; process to finely chop scallions.
2. In a small saucepan, combine scallion, lemon juice, wine, tarragon and chervil. Simmer until mixture is reduced to about 2 tablespoons. Cool.
3. Pour herb mixture into Bowl of Processor. With Blade or Beater Accessory in Bowl, add egg yolks, pepper and butter. Process until thick; about 30 seconds.
4. Pour sauce into the top of a double boiler over warm, not hot water. Keep warm until you are ready to serve.

Makes 1 cup.

VARIATION:
Choron Sauce: Add 1 small tomato, puréed.

Hot Chocolate Sauce

Pour over filled cream puffs (see Index) and ice cream.

8 ounces semi-sweet chocolate
⅔ cup heavy cream or evaporated milk, scalded
¼ teaspoon cinnamon
¼ teaspoon vanilla extract

1. Place Blade in Bowl; with processor running, process the chocolate until it is finely ground.
2. Gradually pour hot cream through the Feed Tube, add vanilla and cinnamon. Process until smooth.
3. Serve immediately.

Makes 1½ cups.

Cranberry and Orange Sauce

Serve hot or cold with poultry or fish.

½ cup sugar
2 teaspoons cornstarch
½ cup orange juice
½ cup water
1 cup raw cranberries
Rind of ½ medium orange

1. Combine sugar, cornstarch, orange juice and water in a 2-quart saucepan; stir until dissolved. Cook, stirring constantly, until mixture comes to a boil.
2. Place Blade in Bowl; process cranberries until finely chopped; add to mixture in saucepan.
3. Process orange rind until finely chopped and add to mixture.

Makes about 1¼ cups.

Holiday Cranberry Sauce

Serve with holiday turkey, duck, goose or chicken.

1 (10-ounce) package cranberries, stemmed
1 (2-inch) piece fresh horseradish, or 2 teaspoons prepared horseradish

2 cups sour cream
1 cup sugar

1. Place Blade in Bowl; process cranberries and horseradish until finely ground.
2. Add sour cream and sugar; blend.
3. Refrigerate until you are ready to serve.

Makes 3 cups.

Dill Sauce

Serve with fish, especially salmon.

¼ cup fresh parsley leaves
6 tablespoons butter or margarine, cut in 1-inch pieces
6 tablespoons flour
2 cups milk

⅛ teaspoon paprika
¾ teaspoon dillweed
Salt to taste
⅛ teaspoon basil
⅛ teaspoon oregano

1. Place Blade in Bowl: process to finely chop parsley. Add remaining ingredients and blend.
2. Pour into a saucepan and cook over low heat until thick, stirring constantly.

Makes 2 cups.

Hollandaise Sauce

Serve over broccoli, asparagus and other cooked green vegetables; also meats and fish.

4 egg yolks
2 tablespoons lemon juice
Salt to taste

Pinch of cayenne pepper
1 cup butter or margarine, melted

1. Place Blade in Bowl: add egg yolks, lemon juice, salt and pepper. Process 3 or 4 seconds until yolks are beaten.
2. With processor running, slowly pour butter through the Feed Tube, processing just until blended.
3. Warm slowly in top of double boiler over hot water, stirring constantly, until mixture is thick.

Makes 1¼ cups.

Mushroom Sauce

Serve with meats or fish.

8 ounces mushrooms
¼ cup butter or margarine
1 medium onion, quartered
1 cup chicken broth

2 tablespoons flour
¼ cup Madeira or sherry wine
Salt and pepper to taste

1. Place Blade in Bowl; process mushrooms until coarsely chopped.
2. Sauté in butter until tender.
3. Process onion until finely chopped. Add broth, flour and wine. Add seasonings to onion; process to blend.
4. Pour into mushrooms in the skillet. Cook, stirring constantly, until mixture boils and thickens.

Makes about 2 cups.

Pesto Sauce

Serve with Ravioli (see Index).

4 cups fresh basil leaves
3 cloves garlic
½ cup pine nuts
½ cup Italian parsley

1 teaspoon salt
½ to 1 cup olive oil
½ cup Pecorino or Parmesan cheese

1. Place Blade in Bowl; add basil, garlic, pine nuts, parsley and salt with ½ cup olive oil.
2. Process, adding enough additional oil to make a smooth paste.
3. Add the cheese and process a few seconds longer.

Makes about 2 cups.

Remoulade Sauce

Serve with crabmeat or other seafood salads.

1 small rib celery, cut in pieces
4 scallions, cut in 1-inch lengths
¼ cup fresh parsley leaves
¼ cup tarragon vinegar
2 tablespoons prepared brown mustard

1 tablespoon catsup
1½ teaspoons paprika
½ teaspoon salt
¼ teaspoon cayenne pepper
½ cup vegetable oil

1. Place Blade in Bowl; process celery, scallions and parsley until finely chopped.
2. Add remaining ingredients except oil to Bowl; with processor running, add oil slowly.
3. Refrigerate 3 to 4 hours to allow flavors to combine properly.

Makes 1¼ cups.

Tampa Sauce

Serve hot with broiled or poached seafood

¼ green pepper, cut into 1-inch pieces	½ cup sugar
Rind from 1 navel orange	½ cup catsup
1 can (6-ounce) frozen orange juice	1½ tablespoons cornstarch
	1 cup water

1. Place Blade in Bowl; process green pepper and navel orange until finely chopped.
2. Combine remaining ingredients in Bowl and process until blended.
3. Pour into a small saucepan and cook until mixture boils, stirring constantly. Lower heat and cook about 5 minutes until sauce thickens and is clear.

Makes 2 cups.

Fresh Tomato Sauce

This sauce may be refrigerated in covered containers for up to 2 weeks, or frozen for as long as 3 months. Serve with spaghetti and meatballs.

1 small onion, quartered	1 tablespoon flour
1 small carrot, cut in 1-inch pieces	1 can (6-ounce) tomato paste
1 celery rib, cut in 1-inch pieces	½ teaspoon oregano
3 tablespoons butter or margarine	½ teaspoon thyme
3 medium ripe tomatoes, quartered	

1. Place Blade in Bowl; process onion, carrot and celery until finely chopped.
2. In a large skillet, brown vegetables in butter about 5 minutes. Add flour.
3. Replace Blade in Bowl. Process tomatoes until puréed; add to the skillet along with the tomato paste and seasonings. Partially cover and simmer until sauce is thickened, about ½ hour.

Makes 3 to 4 cups.

Use on sandwiches, broiled meat or fish, or on crackers. These butters can be stored for a week in the refrigerator. Do not overprocess.

Anchovy Butter

Spread on broiled fish or meat, or use as an appetizer on crackers.

6 anchovy fillets	¾ cup unsalted butter or margarine, softened
1 teaspoon lemon juice	
⅛ teaspoon cayenne pepper	

1. Place Blade in Bowl. Add anchovy fillets, lemon juice and pepper; pulse on and off until finely minced. Scrape down bowl.
2. Add butter; process just to blend.

Makes about ¾ cup.

Cheese Butter

Spread on French Bread, or serve with broiled chops, fish or chicken

1 large clove garlic
4 ounces sharp Cheddar cheese
Dash of hot pepper sauce

½ cup unsalted butter or
margarine, softened

1. Place Blade in Bowl. With processor running, drop garlic cloves through the Feed Tube; process until finely minced.
2. Add cheese, pepper and butter, process until smooth.

Makes about 1½ cups.

Herb Butter

¼ pound butter or margarine,
softened
8 sprigs parsley

1 clove garlic
2 teaspoons chives

Place Blade in Bowl. Add ingredients. Pulse on and off until smooth.

Makes 10 servings.

Parsley Butter

Wrap this butter in foil, freeze and serve with fish, meat or vegetables as the need arises.

1 cup loosely packed parsley leaves
1½ cups butter or margarine,
softened

4 teaspoons lemon juice
Salt and pepper to taste

1. Place Blade in Bowl; process parsley until finely chopped.
2. Add butter, lemon juice, salt and pepper. Process just to blend.

Makes about 1½ cups.

Stuffing for Fish

Stuffings may be used to fill the cavity of a fish just before it is put into the oven for baking, or as a bed on which to put fish fillets for cooking. Generally, plan on 1 cup, or less, of stuffing per pound of fish.

If the stuffing is used to fill a whole fish, the fish should be boned, dried inside and out, sprinkled with salt and pepper, and coated with ½ tablespoon of vegetable oil. The opening should be closed with small skewers or wooden toothpicks; clean string can be laced across the wooden picks as added insurance that the stuffing will stay inside. Bake in a 375° F. oven for about 10 minutes per pound, or until thickest part flakes easily with a fork and the flesh is white.

1 small onion
1 rib celery, cut in 1-inch lengths
6 tablespoons butter or margarine
6 slices dry bread, in pieces

½ cup fresh parsley leaves,
  loosely packed
Salt and pepper to taste
1 teaspoon thyme or sage

1. Place Blade in Bowl; process onion and celery until finely chopped.
2. In a large skillet, sauté onion and celery in butter until tender.
3. Place Blade in Bowl; process bread and parsley until finely crumbed.
4. Add to onion and celery along with seasonings. Mix thoroughly; add a tablespoon of water, milk, fish stock or lemon juice if stuffing is too dry.

VARIATIONS:

1. Omit herbs and add ½ cup chopped nuts.
2. Add 1 medium chopped carrot and 1½ cups spinach or chard leaves, sliced and sautéed until wilted.
3. Add 4 ounces Parmesan cheese, grated.

Makes 5 cups.

Stuffing for Roast Poultry

This recipe makes enough stuffing for an average-sized turkey. Use about ½ for roast chicken.

8 ounces dry bread, in pieces
1 large onion, cut in eighths
3 ribs celery, cut into 1-inch pieces
1 cup packed fresh parsley
Salt and pepper to taste

1½ teaspoons sage
½ teaspoon thyme leaves
½ cup butter or margarine
1 egg
⅔ cup chicken broth

1. Place Blade in Bowl; process about 4 slices of bread at a time to coarse crumbs. As processed, remove to a large bowl.
2. Replace Blade in Bowl; process onion, celery and parsley until finely chopped.
3. Heat butter in skillet and add vegetables and seasonings. Cook over low heat about 10 minutes.
4. Add vegetables to bread crumbs and mix well; stir in egg and broth.

Makes about 8 cups.

Appetizers

Any food that's easy to prepare, is served in small helpings, and stimulates the appetite is suitable as an appetizer. Some are to be found in other chapters of this book, so consider as possibilities such recipes as Marinated Mushrooms, Pickled Beets, Devilled Crab and Kielbasa Sausage Patties.

Choose according to what will follow, giving consideration to flavor, texture and temperature. Generally, a pleasing contrast is desirable. If your main course is hot, serve a cold hors d'oeuvre; a soft textured main dish would be ideally preceded by a crisp first course. If a big dinner is to follow, keep the appetizers light and cocktail time short.

The recipes in this chapter are varied to please every palate. Some can be held in your fingers while standing and visiting; others require a small plate and fork and a place to sit. All of them take little time and effort using your food processor.

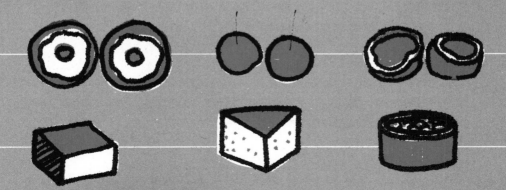

Antipasto Platter

This classic Italian appetizer would be a good first course with Gnocchi (see Index).

4 firm ripe tomatoes, halved
2 large carrots
1 small green pepper, halved
1 small onion
½ pound large fresh mushrooms
½ pound salami, cut to fit
   Feed Tube

½ pound cooked ham, cut to fit
   Feed Tube
8 large pitted ripe olives
8 scallions
8 anchovy fillets
1 (4-ounce) can pimientos
6 teaspoons capers

1. Place Disc, slice side up, in Bowl; slice vegetables and salami and ham. As they are sliced, arrange them on a serving platter with olives, scallions, anchovies, pimientos and capers.
2. Serve with oil and vinegar dressing and crusty Italian bread.

Makes 8 servings.

Avocado Dip

Be careful to process this mixture briefly, so it is a bit lumpy. Serve with celery sticks, cucumber slices, radishes or corn chips.

1 small onion, quartered
¼ cup parsley leaves
1 ripe avocado, peeled and seeded
1 small chili pepper

2 tablespoons white vinegar or
   lemon juice
1 cup mayonnaise (see Index)
Salt and pepper to taste

1. Place Blade in Bowl; add all ingredients and blend, scraping the sides as necessary with a rubber spatula.
2. Transfer to a bowl; cover with waxed paper touching the top to prevent darkening. Refrigerate until ready to serve.

Makes about 2 cups.

Anchovy Stuffed Eggs

1 cup parsley leaves
1 medium onion, quartered
1 (2-ounce) can anchovy fillets
10 hard-cooked eggs
Sour cream

1. Place Blade in Bowl; process parsley until finely chopped and set aside. Add onion, and anchovy fillets. Process until smooth.
2. Cut eggs into halves. Put yolks in Bowl; process to blend. Add as much sour cream as is needed to bind the mixture.
3. Spoon filling into egg halves, and garnish with chopped parsley.

Makes 12 servings.

Caponata

A zesty Mediterranean relish, usually served cold. It keeps refrigerated 4 or 5 days.

1 medium eggplant, unpeeled
  and cut to fit Feed Tube
3 tablespoons vegetable oil
2 large celery ribs, cut in
  1-inch pieces
1 large onion, quartered

2 medium tomatoes quartered
15 stuffed green olives
4 tablespoons red wine vinegar
1½ teaspoons sugar
1 teaspoon pepper

1. Place French Fry Disc in Bowl: slice eggplant. Sauté strips in oil in a large skillet.
2. Place Blade in Bowl; chop celery and onion coarsely; transfer to skillet and cook until golden.
3. Add tomatoes and olives to Bowl; pulse on and off to coarsely chop. Combine with ingredients in skillet. Add wine vinegar, sugar and pepper.
4. Simmer mixture stirring frequently, for 15 minutes.
5. Remove to a bowl, cover and refrigerate. Serve on lettuce or endive with pieces of pita bread (see Index).

Makes about 4 cups.

Snappy Chili Dip

South of the border dip to be served with taco chips, breadsticks, or celery or cucumber sticks.

1 clove garlic
1 can (4-ounces) green chilies
1 large green pepper, seeded
   and quartered
1 can (28-ounces) tomatoes,
   drained

1 small onion, quartered
2 tablespoons chili powder
½ teaspoon each, cumin and
   coriander seeds

1. Place Blade in Bowl; add all ingredients and process until smooth.
2. Transfer mixture to a crock; refrigerate at least 8 hours.

Makes 4 cups.

Hummus (Chick Pea Spread)

A Middle Eastern spread you can whip up in minutes and keep refrigerated for days before the party.

2 garlic cloves, peeled
3 scallions, cut in 1-inch lengths
1 can (20-ounces) chick peas,
   drained
1 can (15-ounces) tahini
   (sesame butter)

Juice of 2 large lemons
⅔ cup water
Salt and pepper to taste
Parsley for garnish

1. Place Blade in Bowl. With processor running, drop garlic cloves and scallions through Feed Tube; add remaining ingredients. Process until the mixture is smooth and creamy.
2. Transfer to a serving bowl. Garnish with parsley. Cover and chill. Serve at room temperature with lightly heated triangles of pita bread (see Index).

Makes about 1½ cups.

Potted Cheese and Wine

The English call foods "potted" when small amounts of cheese, fish or meat are mixed with seasonings and packed into a crock.

1 pound sharp Cheddar or
  Leicester cheese, chilled, cut to
  fit Feed Tube
4 ounces Parmesan cheese
8 ounces butter or margarine,
  chilled and cut into 1-inch cubes

Pinch of cayenne pepper
Pinch of ground mace
4 ounces dry Madeira wine
1 teaspoon Dijon mustard

1. Place Blade in Bowl. Add all ingredients; process until smooth. Press cheese into a crock. Cover with plastic wrap and refrigerate up to several days.
2. Serve at room temperature with whole wheat crackers.

Makes 2½ cups.

Liptauer Cheese

This Hungarian cheese spread has become an American cocktail hour favorite.

8 ounces cottage cheese
⅓ cup of butter or margarine
½ teaspoon anchovy paste
1 tablespoon capers
1 tablespoon caraway seeds

2 tablespoons minced chives
1 tablespoon prepared mustard
1 tablespoon paprika
Salt to taste
1 clove garlic, halved

1. Place Blade in Bowl. Process the cottage cheese and butter together until well blended. Add remaining ingredients except salt and garlic. Blend until smooth. Add salt to taste.
2. Rub a serving bowl with the cut clove of garlic and pack cheese into it. Chill at least 5 hours before serving. Serve with cocktail rye or dark pumpernickel.

About 1½ cups.

Chutney Cheese Dip

The flavor of India adds interest to this dip. It may be kept in the refrigerator for several days.

1 garlic clove
1 medium onion, quartered
2 tablespoons butter or margarine
1 tablespoon curry powder
⅓ cup peach chutney (see Index)

2 tablespoons light cream
1 package (8-ounce) cream cheese
   cut in 1-inch pieces
Dash black pepper

1. Place Blade in Bowl. With processor running, drop garlic cloves through Feed Tube; process until finely minced. Pulse on and off to finely chop onion.
2. In a small skillet sauté onion and garlic in butter. Replace Blade in Bowl. Add remaining ingredients. Process just to blend.
3. Transfer to a small bowl. Cover and refrigerate.
4. To serve, surround the dip with crisp celery, carrot sticks, zucchini, green pepper and other raw vegetables that can be used to scoop it up.

Makes 1½ cups.

Crab Meat Puffs

A good filling for Pâté à Chou (see Index).

½ cup mayonnaise
¼ cup lemon juice or
   cider vinegar
1 scallion, cut in 1-inch
   pieces
1 slice unpeeled lime or
   lemon
¼ teaspoon salt
⅛ teaspoon pepper

2 drops hot pepper sauce
1 tablespoon drained capers
2 (6-ounce each) packages
   frozen crab meat, thawed and
   drained or 2 cans (6½ or
   7½-ounce each), boned and
   flaked
Cream puff shells (see Index)

1. Place Blade in Bowl; add mayonnaise, lemon juice or vinegar, scallion, lime and seasonings. Process until scallion and lime are finely chopped. Add crab meat; blend
2. Cut tops from cream puff shells. Fill bottom halves with crab meat mixture; cover with tops.

About 16 portions.

Herring Paté

A little of this goes a long way to stimulate appetites.

1 jar (12-ounce) herring in
    wine sauce, drained
1 package (8-ounce) cream cheese
½ cup pitted ripe olives

1 cup parsley, loosely packed
½ teaspoon curry powder
Juice of half a lemon

1. Place Blade in Bowl; add all ingredients and process until smooth—about a minute.
2. Transfer mixture to a crock. Cover and chill until ready to serve. Serve with dark rye or pumpernickle bread.

Makes 3 cups.

Potted Shrimp

This traditional English recipe is a tasty way to begin a meal. It may be made a week ahead of time and refrigerated.

1 pound shrimp, cooked, shelled
    and deveined
1 small onion, quartered
Worcestershire sauce

Celery salt
Cayenne pepper
½ cup butter or margarine

1. Place Blade in Bowl; pulse on and off about 5 times to chop shrimp. Add remaining ingredients and purée until smooth.
2. Remove to an earthenware pot and chill until ready to serve. Serve with melba toast.

Makes about 1½ cups.

Smoked Salmon Paté

A delectable spread.

4 ounces heavy cream
8 ounces smoked Nova Scotia
    salmon, cut in small pieces
2 tablespoons unsalted butter or
    margarine

1 teaspoon lemon juice
White pepper to taste
2 teaspoons capers

1. Place Beater Accessory in Bowl; whip cream until it peaks.
2. Place Blade in another Bowl; process salmon, lemon juice and pepper until puréed. Add whipped cream and mix to blend.
3. Pack into a glass serving bowl; sprinkle with capers. Cover with plastic wrap and refrigerate. Serve with assorted crackers.

Makes 1½ cups.

Salmon Mousse

This light spread looks very attractive in a fish-shaped mold, decorated with cucumber slices.

1 envelope unflavored gelatin
¼ cup cold water
2 tablespoons lemon juice
½ cup mayonnaise
1 small onion, halved
2 ribs celery, cut in 1-inch pieces
1 can (16-ounce) red salmon, drained

⅛ teaspoon paprika
½ teaspoon dill weed
1 tablespoon catsup
1 tablespoon cream cheese
½ cup parsley leaves
1 cup heavy cream
1 cucumber, peeled

1. Sprinkle gelatin over cold water in the top of a double boiler. Let stand a few minutes to soften. Place over boiling water; stir gelatin until it is dissolved. Add lemon juice and mayonnaise; blend well.
2. Place Blade in Bowl; process onion, celery, and salmon until finely chopped. Add mayonnaise mixture, paprika, dill, catsup, cream cheese and parsley; blend.
3. Place Beater Accessory in a clean Bowl. Whip cream until stiff. Fold whipped cream into salmon mixture.
4. Spread into a lightly oiled 4-cup mold; chill until set, about 2 hours. Unmold and serve with dark rye bread rounds, or crisp crackers.

Makes 16 servings.

Steak Tartare Deluxe

The processor makes this sophisticated hors d' oeuvre in short order. Make it at the last moment, and use only the very freshest meat.

2 pounds tenderloin
  steak, cut into 1-inch cubes
1 medium onion, quartered
10 anchovy fillets

2 egg yolks
1 teaspoon salt
½ teaspoon pepper
1 tablespoon Dijon mustard

1. Place Blade in Bowl; process ingredients until finely chopped. Remove to a mixing bowl, cover and chill.
2. Serve in a mound with crackers or bread.

Makes 8 to 10 servings.

Seviche

This seafood cocktail appears in a variety of versions in Mexico and Latin America.

2 large cloves garlic
Rind of 1 lemon
1 large Spanish onion, quartered
2 pounds sea scallops or other
　white fish, partially frozen
1½ cups fresh lemon juice
1 bunch scallions, cut in
　1-inch lengths

2 medium tomatoes, quartered
1 or 2 hot peppers with seeds
　removed (optional) or a few
　drops hot pepper sauce
Salt
Lettuce leaves

1. Place Blade in Bowl. With processor running, drop garlic and lemon rind through Feed Tube. Process until finely minced. Add onion and finely chop.
2. Place Disc, slice side up, in Bowl; slice the fish. Transfer contents to a shallow glass bowl; add enough lemon juice to cover, stirring with a fork until juice is almost completely absorbed. Let stand 20 minutes until mixture turns white. Stir occasionally.
3. Place Blade in Bowl; process scallions, tomatoes and hot peppers until coarsely chopped. Stir into fish mixture. Add salt to taste.
4. Cover the bowl and let the mixture marinate at least 6 hours, stirring occasionally.
5. Before serving, drain off excess liquid. Serve on lettuce leaves with corn chips.

Makes 10 to 12 servings.

Chicken Liver Mousse

A rich brandy-flavored spread.

1 shallot or small onion
1 clove garlic
½ cup unsalted butter or
　margarine, softened
1 pound chicken livers,
　trimmed

½ teaspoon salt
¼ teaspoon ground pepper
⅛ teaspoon nutmeg
2 tablespoons Brandy
⅔ cup heavy cream*
Paprika

1. Place Blade in Bowl; process to finely chop shallot or onion and garlic clove. In a large skillet, melt ¼ cup of the butter; sauté onion, garlic until transparent. Cook livers until browned, but still pink inside. Add seasonings and brandy; allow to cool.
2. Place Beater Accessory in Bowl; whip cream until it forms stiff peaks.
3. Place Blade in Bowl; add livers and remaining butter. Pulse on and off until puréed. Transfer to a bowl, fold in the whipped cream and press plastic wrap directly onto the surface of the mousse. Refrigerate for at least 4 hours. Serve spread on melba toast or rye bread rounds. Sprinkle with paprika.

Makes 2 cups.

* For a firmer mousse, replace cream with an additional ½ cup butter.

Chicken Liver Paté

An old fashioned favorite paté.

3 cups water
6 sprigs fresh parsley
1 rib celery with leaves
8 peppercorns
¼ teaspoon tarragon
½ pound chicken livers
1 small onion, quartered
1 clove garlic

8 tablespoons butter or
  margarine
½ teaspoon salt
Dash cayenne pepper
1 teaspoon dry mustard
½ teaspoon nutmeg
2 hard-cooked eggs
2 tablespoons melted butter

1. Bring water to boiling in a medium saucepan; add parsley, celery, peppercorns and tarragon. Simmer 5 minutes and add chicken livers; cover and cook 10 minutes. Allow to cool.
2. Place Blade in Bowl. Chop onion coarsely. With motor running, drop garlic through Feed Tube to mince. Sauté onion and garlic in the butter in a small skillet until golden brown.
3. Replace Blade in Bowl; add the livers, salt, pepper, mustard, nutmeg and eggs. Process until mixture is smooth. Pour into a terrine and cover with melted butter; chill. Mixture is thin, but will become firm when chilled.
4. Serve with assorted crackers.

Makes about 1¼ cups.

Tuna Paté

Substitute minced clams or crab meat for the tuna.

2 (3-ounce) packages cream cheese,
  cut in 1-inch pieces
2 hard-cooked eggs
1 (7-ounce) can tuna fish, in oil

12 Greek black olives
1½ teaspoons capers
Pepper to taste

1. Place Blade in Bowl; process cream cheese until smooth; add eggs and tuna with oil; blend. Add olives and capers; pulse on and off a few times to coarsely chop olives. Season to taste.
2. Pack the paté into a bowl; garnish with slices of olive or capers. Chill and serve with melba toast.

Makes 1½ cups.

Tiny Cheese Wafers

These crisp cheese snacks always disappear rapidly.

**8 ounces Cheddar or Swiss Cheese,
  chilled and cut into 1-inch cubes**
**1 cup butter or margarine, chilled
  and cubed**

2 cups flour
Salt and pepper to taste
Paprika

1. Place Blade in Bowl; process cheese and butter; add flour, salt and pepper through the Feed Tube. Wrap dough in waxed paper and chill at least 3 hours.
2. Form into small balls; place on a cookie sheet, and sprinkle with paprika.
3. Bake in a preheated 400° F oven for 10 minutes or until lightly browned. Serve hot.

Makes about 50 portions.

Codfish Cakes

An old American favorite, made easily in the processor.

1 pound salt codfish
**4 to 5 medium potatoes, peeled and
  halved**

1 egg
½ teaspoon pepper
2 tablespoons vegetable oil

1. Soak fish in cold water to cover overnight. Drain.
2. Place Disc, slice side up, in Bowl. Slice potatoes, and place them in a saucepan of cold water. Place the salt cod on top, and boil for about 20 minutes, or until the potatoes are tender. Drain. Break the cod into pieces after picking out bone and gristle.
3. Place Blade in Bowl. Chop codfish and potatoes until well blended. Empty into a mixing bowl, add the eggs and pepper. Stir well and chill to firm the mixture.
4. Using a teaspoon, scoop up spoonfuls, and flatten with a fork to make them "whiskery." Fry in vegetable oil over moderate heat, turning once until golden on both sides. Spear with toothpicks, and serve hot with chili sauce.

Makes 24 portions.

Escargots (Snails) in Garlic Tomato Sauce

Break your budget for an elegant beginning to a gala evening.

8 shallots
8 cloves garlic
5 cans (60) French snails

1 teaspoon thyme
2 cups dry white wine

1. Place Blade in Bowl. Pulse on and off to chop shallots and garlic cloves. In a saucepan, combine with remaining ingredients and bring to full boil.
2. Remove from heat, allow to cool down and refrigerate for at least 8 hours.

SAUCE:

6 garlic cloves, peeled
8 shallots, peeled
¾ pound mushrooms
10 fresh plum tomatoes

Salt and ground pepper to
   taste
4 ounces butter or margarine
1 cup brandy
1 pint heavy cream

1. Place Blade in Bowl. With processor running, drop garlic cloves and shallots through Feed Tube; process until finely chopped; add mushrooms and plum tomatoes; process until finely chopped; set aside.
2. Drain and wipe off marinated snails.
3. Heat butter in a saucepan over medium heat. Add chopped garlic, shallots, mushrooms and tomatoes; stir. Add the snails and brandy. Simmer until dry. Add cream; stir until thick. Serve in ramekins or small bowls.

Makes 6 servings.

Spinach Cheese Bites

A warm welcome to start the party.

**1 pound fresh spinach,
    stemmed**
**½ pound Parmesan cheese, cut
    in cubes**

8 ounces water chestnuts
1½ cups mayonnaise
½ teaspoon grated nutmeg
Rye bread rounds

1. Wash and cook spinach in water left on leaves for 5 minutes.
2. Place Disc, shred side up, in Bowl. Process to shred Parmesan. Remove Disc and place Blade in Bowl; add water chestnuts and spinach. Process until finely chopped. Add mayonnaise and nutmeg. Process just to mix.
3. Transfer to a bowl, cover and refrigerate.
4. To serve, spread on bread slices and place under the broiler until bubbly.

Makes 36 portions.

Parmesan Stuffed Mushrooms

You could substitute for the chopped mushrooms, 1 cup chopped crab meat or chopped shrimps and add 1 teaspoon of chopped dill to the herbs.

**16 large mushrooms, stems
    reserved**
1 small onion, peeled and halved
8 tablespoons butter or margarine
1 cup loosely packed parsley leaves

1 slice dry bread, in pieces
2 eggs lightly beaten
¼ teaspoon hot pepper sauce
1 teaspoon ground black pepper
2 ounces Parmesan cheese

1. Place Blade in Bowl; process stems and onion until finely chopped. In a large skillet, sauté the chopped mushroom stems and onion in 4 tablespoons of the butter.
2. Process parsley and bread until finely chopped; add to the mushroom stems and onion. Blend in eggs and seasonings.
3. Place Disc, shred side up, in Bowl. Shred cheese.
4. Replace Blade and process cheese until finely grated; set aside.
5. Melt remaining butter and dip each mushroom cap in it; place them in a 9x12-inch baking pan, flat side down. Fill caps with the mixture and sprinkle with Parmesan cheese.
6. Bake in a preheated 400 ° F. oven for 10 minutes. Serve hot.

Makes 16 portions.

Salmon Turnovers

Filled pastries that may be prepared and frozen until you are ready to heat and serve them.

1 small onion, quartered
1 (2-inch) piece fresh horseradish, peeled
4 slices crisply fried bacon
Hot pepper sauce

1 (16-ounce) can salmon, drained, bones removed
¾ cup condensed Cheddar cheese soup
Cream Cheese pastry (see Index)

1. Place Blade in Bowl. Pulse on and off a few times to chop onions and horseradish. Add remaining ingredients and process just until mixed. Chill.
2. Roll Cream Cheese Pastry thin and cut into 2½ inch squares. Place a heaping teaspoonful of the filling on half of each square. Fold over and press edges with a fork. Place turnovers on cookie sheets.
3. Bake 20 to 25 minutes in a preheated 450° F. oven.

Makes 24 portions.

Chinese Cocktail Meatballs

Tempting hors d'oeuvres with a Far East flavor.

1 pound beef, cut in cubes
½ cup water chestnuts
2 scallions, cut in 1-inch pieces
¼ teaspoon ginger

3 tablespoons soy sauce
2 tablespoons water
Pepper
2 tablespoons vegetable oil

1. Place Blade in Bowl. Add meat, water chestnuts and scallions; process on and off to chop, then run continuously until finely ground. Add ginger, soy sauce, water and pepper; blend.
2. Shape into bite-sized meatballs. Chill 1 hour in freezer.
3. Heat oil in skillet and brown meatballs on all sides. Serve hot with toothpicks.

Makes 12 portions.

Soups

Although most soups are served before the main course, some are hearty enough to be the main course. And in Scandinavian countries, fruit soups are sometimes served as dessert.

The soups in this chapter can be prepared ahead of time to be chilled or reheated. With your processor to do the chopping and slicing, there is very little work involved, so they are almost as convenient as canned soups and far tastier and more aromatic when they are homemade.

Apple Bisque

It was a cold winter night when we tasted this soup at Annie B's restaurant in Boston. Chef Kayo Oliveira was kind enough to share the recipe and also wishes you "Boa Sorte" ("Good Luck" in Portuguese).

1 medium onion, quartered
2 tablespoons butter or
  margarine
2 medium parsnips, peeled
2 large white turnips, peeled,
  cut to fit Feed Tube

2 medium apples, peeled,
  cored and halved
4 cups chicken broth
½ cup long grain rice
Salt and pepper to taste
1 cup apple cider
1 cup light cream

1. Place Blade in Bowl; process onion until finely chopped. Sauté onions in butter in a 6-quart heavy kettle, until soft.
2. Place Disc, slice side up, in Bowl. Slice parsnips, turnips, and apples; add to the onions along with rice and broth. Simmer for 1 hour, until vegetables are tender.
3. Set a colander over a large mixing bowl and pour contents of the pan through. Pour the liquid into the pan.
4. Place Blade in Bowl. Process the soup vegetables to a smooth purée. Season; add the purée to the liquid in the pan. Add cider and cream. Reheat slowly, stirring occasionally.

Makes 6 servings.

Cabbage Borscht

There are endless variations to this hearty Russian soup, but they all have beets.

1 pound beef chuck with
   bones
2 quarts water
1 large head cabbage, cut to
   fit Feed Tube
5 fresh beets, peeled
2 medium onions, quartered

1 can (28-ounce) tomatoes
¼ cup brown sugar
Juice of 1 lemon
Salt to taste
¼ teaspoon ginger
1 cup sour cream (optional)

1. In a 6-quart pot, simmer meat and bones in water for 30 minutes.
2. Meanwhile, place Disc, shred side up, in Bowl; shred cabbage; empty shredded cabbage into a large mixing bowl.
3. Reverse Disc to slice side up. Slice beets and onions. Add cabbage, beets, onions, tomatoes, brown sugar, lemon juice, salt and ginger to the pot. Simmer, covered, for 2 hours.
4. With tongs, remove meat, discard bones, and cut away any remaining fat on meat.
5. Place Blade in Bowl; pulse on and off a few times to coarsely chop meat, and return meat to soup. Serve hot with dollops of sour cream.

Makes 16 servings.

Swedish Cabbage Soup

A bowl of this hot soup is the answer to winters in Sweden.

1 large head cabbage, cored
   and cut into wedges
¼ cup butter or margarine
3 tablespoons brown sugar

4 cups beef bouillon
1 teaspoon salt
½ teaspoon pepper
¼ teaspoon ground allspice

1. Place Disc, slice side up, in Bowl. Slice cabbage.
2. In a 4-quart deep saucepan, brown cabbage in butter until light brown. Add sugar and cook, stirring until sugar is dissolved. Add beef bouillon, salt, pepper and allspice. Simmer, covered, for about 1 hour.

Makes 6 to 8 servings.

Cream of Cauliflower Soup

Another simple and delicious soup for a cold winter's day.

1 medium cauliflower, separated
   into flowerets
1 medium carrot
4 cups milk

2 tablespoons butter or margarine
2 tablespoons flour
Salt and pepper to taste

1. Cook the cauliflower in water until tender, about 5 to 7 minutes. Drain.
2. Place Blade in Bowl; add carrot and grate. Empty onto waxed paper. Pour ½ cup of the milk into the Bowl; add the cauliflower, butter, flour and seasoning. Process until puréed.
3. Pour the mixture into a large saucepan. Heat thoroughly, stirring continuously.
4. Serve soup hot, garnished with grated carrot.

Makes 6 to 8 servings.

Italian Minestrone Soup

For a one-dish meal, this soup should be served with good bread like Tomato Gruyere Bread (see Index).

1½ ounces Parmesan cheese,
   cut in 1-inch pieces
1 medium onion, quartered
1 medium carrot, cut in 1-inch
   pieces
2 stalks celery, cut in 1-inch
   pieces
¼ cup vegetable oil
2 cups bottled clam juice
2 cups water

1 can (2 pounds, 3-ounce) plum
   tomatoes
2 cups thin noodles, uncooked
½ teaspoon oregano
½ teaspoon Italian seasoning
½ teaspoon garlic powder
Salt and pepper
2 pounds fish fillets, cut
   into bite-size pieces

1. Place Disc, shred side up, in Bowl; shred Parmesan cheese.
2. Process to coarsely chop onion, carrot and celery.
3. In a medium saucepan, sauté vegetables in oil until tender. Add clam juice, water, tomatoes, noodles and seasonings. Simmer covered, 30 minutes. Add fish to soup and simmer until fish flakes easily when tested with a fork, about 10 minutes. Serve with grated Parmesan cheese.

Makes 6 servings.

French Onion Soup

A flavorful soup to begin a meat or fish dinner.

6 medium onions
4 tablespoons butter or margarine
4 cans (10½ ounces each) beef
    consommé, undiluted

6 ounces Parmesan cheese, cubed
4 to 6 slices French bread,
    1-inch thick
Salt and pepper to taste

1. Place Disc, slice side up, in Bowl; process to thinly slice onion.
2. Heat butter in a medium saucepan. Add onion and sauté, stirring, until golden, over moderate heat for about 10 minutes. Add consommé and simmer, covered, about 30 minutes.
3. While onion is cooking, reverse Disc to shred side up; shred Parmesan. Place Blade in Bowl; process Parmesan until finely grated.
4. Toast bread slices. Sprinkle one side of each with some grated cheese. Put under broiler 1 minute, or until cheese is bubbly.
5. To serve, ladle soup into individual soup bowls. Float toasted bread, cheese side up, on soup. Sprinkle additional grated cheese on top.

Makes 4 to 6 servings

Cream of Spinach Soup

A good supper soup to reheat and serve with assorted cheeses and crackers.

1 package (10-ounces) fresh
    spinach rinsed and stemmed
1 medium onion, quartered
¼ cup butter or margarine

¼ cup of flour
4 cups milk
Salt and pepper to taste
Croutons

1. Cook spinach about 5 minutes in the water remaining on the leaves.
2. Place Blade in Bowl. Process to finely chop onion. In a 1½-quart saucepan, cook onion in butter; stir in flour. Cook until bubbly; slowly add milk. Cook, stirring constantly, until thickened. Do not boil.
3. Replace Blade in Bowl; finely chop spinach. Stir chopped spinach and seasonings into the soup. Let stand about 15 minutes. Serve garnished with croutons.

Makes 6 servings.

Fresh Tomato Soup

Use only the freshest home grown tomatoes for this soup to get the fullest flavor.

1 (2-inch) strip lemon rind
1½ tablespoons sugar
1 medium onion, quartered
¼ cup parsley leaves
5 medium tomatoes, halved

2 teaspoons paprika
Salt to taste
2 cups milk
Lemon juice to taste

1. Place Blade in Bowl. Add lemon rind and sugar. Process to finely grate lemon rind. With processor running, drop onion and parsley through Feed Tube, mince onion and parsley. Remove to a medium saucepan.
2. Place Disc, slice side up, in Bowl. Slice tomatoes. Add them to the saucepan along with remaining ingredients. Cook gently about 15 minutes. Do not boil.

Makes 4 servings.

Fresh Vegetable Soup

3 potatoes, peeled and cut
   to fit Feed Tube
2 purple-top turnips, peeled and
   cut to fit Feed Tube
3 carrots
2 ribs celery, cut to fit Feed Tube

Half a small head of cabbage, cut to
   fit Feed Tube
10 cups chicken broth
5 peppercorns
1 cup green beans, cut in 1-inch
   lengths

1. Place Disc, slice side up, in Bowl. Slice the potatoes, turnips, carrots and celery.
2. Reverse Disc to shred side; shred cabbage.
3. In a large pot, combine chicken broth with vegetables and peppercorns. Bring to a boil. Cover and simmer about 1½ hours. Add beans. Simmer about 10 minutes. Serve topped with Herb Butter (see Index).

Makes 10 servings.

Zucchini Cheese Soup

Zucchini is available year round and is suitable, sliced or shredded, in a variety of dishes.

4 ounces Cheddar cheese
2 medium zucchini, cut to fit Feed Tube
1 medium onion, quartered
1 green pepper, seeded and cut in 1-inch pieces
2 pieces pimiento

4 tablespoons butter or margarine
1 cup water
½ teaspoon salt
¼ cup flour
⅛ teaspoon pepper
2½ cups milk
½ teaspoon Worcestershire sauce

1. Place Disc, shred side up, in Bowl. Shred cheese; set aside. Reverse Disc to slice side. Slice zucchini; set aside. Place Blade in Bowl. Chop onion, green pepper and pimiento.
2. Melt half of the butter in a large skillet. Sauté onion, pepper and pimiento until tender. Add zucchini, water and ½ teaspoon salt to the skillet. Cover. Bring to a boil; turn down to simmer and cook about 5 minutes, or until zucchini is tender.
3. Heat remaining butter in a large saucepan; blend in flour and pepper. Remove from heat; gradually stir in milk and Worcestershire sauce. Heat to boiling, stirring constantly. Boil and stir 1 minute. Remove from heat; stir in cheese until melted. Do not boil.
4. Combine cheese sauce with vegetables in the skillet and heat to serving temperature. Additional milk may be added to achieve desired consistency.

Makes 6 servings.

Chilled Avocado Soup

A mild, pleasant-tasting soup, possibly the start of a seafood luncheon menu.

2 large avocados, peeled
   and cubed
Lemon juice
2 cloves garlic

1 medium tomato
2 cups chicken broth
1 cup heavy cream
2 lemons, ends cut off

1. Place Blade in Bowl. Process avocado cubes until smooth. Transfer to a large bowl with lemon juice to prevent avocado from darkening.
2. With processor running, drop garlic cloves through Feed Tube. Process to finely mince garlic. Process tomato, pulsing on and off just until it is chopped.
3. Combine with the avocado, broth and cream in a large bowl. Cover and refrigerate. Before serving, place Disc, slice side up, in Bowl. Slice lemons for garnish.

Makes 6 servings.

Frosty Cucumber Soup

Chill this soup for several hours before serving to let the flavors blend.

4 medium cucumbers, peeled,
   seeded and cut into 1-inch pieces
1 medium onion, quartered
1 avocado, peeled and pitted

2 cups chicken broth
1 cup light cream
Salt and pepper to taste
Paprika or a sprig of fresh dill

1. Put vegetables in broth in a large saucepan and simmer until tender.
2. Place a colander over a large mixing bowl and pour through to drain off liquid.
3. Place Blade in Bowl. Process vegetables and avocado to a smooth purée.
4. Return vegetables and liquid to the pan and season to taste with salt, pepper and puréed avocado; reheat. Stir in the cream. Serve garnished with a dash of paprika or a sprig of fresh dill.

Makes 8 servings.

Senegalese Soup

A North African safari soup. See Index for instructions in preparing coconut.

3 ounces fresh coconut meat
1 cup cooked chicken, cut in
   1-inch pieces
2 onions, quartered
2 ribs celery, cut in 1-inch pieces
2 apples, peeled and quartered
4 tablespoons butter or margarine

2 tablespoons curry powder
¼ teaspoon cinnamon
2 tablespoons flour
1 quart chicken broth
Salt to taste
2 cups heavy cream

1. Place Blade in Bowl. Process to finely chop coconut; set aside. Finely chop chicken; set aside. Finely chop onions, celery and apples.
2. In a large saucepan, cook onions, celery and apples in butter until tender. Add curry powder, cinnamon and flour; cook and stir constantly until thickened. Gradually add chicken broth, stirring until smooth. Add minced chicken and salt, if desired.
3. Chill. Add cream just before serving. Serve very cold with a sprinkling of coconut.

Makes 8 servings.

Strawberry Apple Soup

This fruit soup is typical of those served in Scandinavian countries either as a beginning course or as a desert.

3 medium apples, quartered
1¾ cups water
½ cup sugar
1 stick cinnamon
3 cups apple juice

1 cup pineapple juice
2 teaspoons lemon juice
3 tablespoons cornstarch
1 package (10-ounces) frozen
   strawberries

1. Place Blade in Bowl. Process apples about 45 seconds, or until smooth and puréed. Place puréed apple in a large saucepan. Add 1½ cups of the water, sugar, cinnamon stick, apple juice, pineapple juice and lemon juice. Simmer 10 minutes. Remove cinammon stick.
2. Mix cornstarch with ¼ cup of water. Stir into fruit mixture in saucepan. Simmer 5 minutes, or until slightly thickened and clear.
3. Stir in strawberries; they will thaw almost at once in the liquid. Chill well.

Makes 8 servings.

Manhattan Summer Vegetable Soup

For the busy urban professional, a fresh vegetable soup, made with amazing speed with the processor.

4 medium onions, quartered
2 tablespoons butter or margarine
4 medium tomatoes, peeled, halved
2 large cucumbers, peeled, seeded and cut in 1-inch pieces
2 cups chicken broth

1 teaspoon basil
½ teaspoon ground black pepper
1 teaspoon dill weed
¼ teaspoon thyme
2 cups yogurt
Fresh mint for garnish

1. Place Blade in Bowl. Process to coarsely chop onions.
2. In a large pot, heat butter; sauté onions until transparent.
3. Coarsely chop tomatoes and cucumbers. Add to the onions, along with broth and seasonings. Simmer 30 minutes. Add yogurt and blend well. Refrigerate. Serve cold with mint garnish.

Makes 6 servings.

Meats & Poultry

If you enjoy trying unusual cuisines, you'll be pleased to find here recipes originating from places as divergent as the heartland of America and Japan, China, Italy, Mexico and Greece.

There are everyday and party main dishes, simply prepared foods such as Pork Chops on a Bed of Cabbage and Apples and those requiring a little more effort, like Turkey Cutlets Stuffed with Veal Mousse.

Some of the one-dish meals can be made in advance, for instance, Beef Stroganoff or Mexican Pot Roast. Others like Sukiyaki should be made just before serving.

Your food processor is your best help, when it comes to chopping meat or poultry until it's smooth, as in Baked Mousse of Chicken or Veal Sour Cream Loaf. It's fast and efficient, and makes you wonder how you managed without it.

Spicy Italian Meatballs

Best served over hot spaghetti sprinkled with grated Parmesan cheese.

1½ pounds beef chuck, cut in
  cubes
2 slices of dry bread, in pieces
6 ounces sharp Cheddar cheese,
  cut in 1 inch cubes
1 medium onion, quartered
½ cup loosely packed parsley
  sprigs

2 eggs
⅛ teaspoon salt
¼ teaspoon pepper
⅛ teaspoon oregano
2 tablespoons vegetable oil
Fresh tomato sauce (see Index)

1. Place Blade in Bowl; process beef cubes until finely chopped; remove to
   a large mixing bowl.
2. Process bread, cheese and onion until finely chopped; add to meat along
   with eggs and seasonings.
3. With wet hands, shape meat mixture into small balls, about an inch in
   diameter. In a large skillet, brown meatballs slowly in hot oil.
4. Pour heated Fresh Tomato Sauce (see Index) over meatballs. Cover and
   simmer 10 minutes.

Makes 10 servings.

Midwest Meat Loaf

Bake Au Gratin Potatoes (see Index) at the same time.

3 slices bread, in pieces
½ cup water
1 cup parsley leaves
1 small onion, halved
¾ pound beef, cubed
½ pound lean pork, cubed

½ pound veal, cubed
1 egg
1 teaspoon Worcestershire sauce
1 teaspoon salt
Pepper to taste
2 slices bacon

1. Place Blade in Bowl; process bread to fine crumbs. Transfer to a mixing
   bowl and add water.
2. Replace Blade in Bowl; chop parsley and onion and mix with bread and
   water. Process meats until finely ground, removing each as chopped to
   the mixing bowl.
3. Stir egg, Worcestershire sauce, salt and pepper into the mixture. Pack
   into a 9 x 5 x 3-inch greased loaf pan. Place bacon slices on top.
4. Bake 1½ hours in a 350° F. oven. Serve hot or cold.

Makes 8 servings.

Beef Strogonoff

A glorified version of Russian stew. Serve with hot buttered noodles.

1 pound beef tenderloin
  trimmed and cut to fit
  Feed Tube
1 clove garlic
1 large red onion
6 large fresh mushrooms,
  stemmed
¼ cup buter or margarine

1 tablespoon flour
1 tablespoon tomato paste
2 cups beef broth
Salt and pepper to taste
½ cup sour cream or yogurt
Cooked noodles (see Index)

1. Wrap and partially freeze beef about 1 hour
2. Place Blade in Bowl; with processor running, mince garlic.
3. Place Disc, slice side up, in Bowl; process to slice onion and mushrooms. Empty garlic, onion and mushrooms into a large skillet with 2 tablespoons of the butter; brown.
4. Heat remaining butter in a saucepan; add flour and brown. Add tomato paste, beef broth and seasonings to taste. Cook and stir until the sauce is smooth and boils.
5. Replace Disc, slice side up, in Bowl; slice beef and add slices to the skillet with mushrooms and onions. Quickly brown. Add sauce and simmer 4 or 5 minutes. Stir in sour cream and heat, but do not boil. Serve with cooked noodles.

Makes 4 servings.

Mexican Pot Roast

Serve with pinto beans and tortillas

2 pounds beef chuck steak
2 tablespoons vegetable oil
1 clove garlic
2 medium onions, quartered
3 medium tomatoes, quartered

1 rib celery, cut into small pieces
1 green chili
1 teaspoon chili powder
¼ teaspoon cumin
Salt and pepper

1. Remove fat and bones from chuck steak and cut into 6 servings.
2. Heat oil in large skillet and brown meat on both sides.
3. While meat is browning, place Blade in Bowl. With processor running, drop garlic clove through Feed Tube. Process onions, tomatoes, celery and green chili until coarsely chopped. Add seasonings and pour over meat. Simmer about 2 hours, or until meat is tender.

Makes 4 to 6 servings.

Sukiyaki

Gather family and friends around for delightful Japanese table cooking.

1½ pounds sirloin steak
  cut to fit Feed Tube
4 ribs celery, cut to fit
  Feed Tube
2 large onions, halved lenghtwise
1 bunch scallions
6 large fresh mushrooms
8 ounces fresh spinach, rinsed
  and stemmed

1 can (8½-ounce) bamboo shoots,
  drained
½ cup soy sauce
3 tablespoons white wine
5 tablespoons water
1 tablepsoon sugar
1 tablespoon butter or margarine
Hot cooked rice

1. Put meat in freezer for about an hour to partially freeze.
2. Place Disc, slice side up, in Bowl. Slice meat.
3. Arrange slices down the center of a large platter. Cover with plastic wrap and refrigerate.
4. Slice celery, onions, scallions and mushrooms.
5. Steam spinach 1 minute in a colander over boiling water.
6. Arrange vegetables in rows on either side of the meat. Again, cover with plastic wrap and refrigerate.
7. Combine soy sauce, wine, water and sugar in a small pitcher.
8. In a large skillet, melt butter; add ⅓ of the meat and pour ⅔ of the sauce over the meat. Add ⅔ of the assorted vegetables to the skillet. Cook and stir gently about 6 minutes. Add another ⅓ of the meat and cook a few minutes longer. Serve in bowls or small plates with hot cooked rice.
9. To prepare "seconds," add remainder of meat and vegetables and sauce as needed for moisture. Cook 7 minutes, stirring constantly.

Makes 4 servings.

Tacos

¼ large head iceberg lettuce
1 medium tomato, quartered
1 clove garlic
1 small onion, quartered
2 tablespoons oil
1 pound lean beef, cut in 1-inch cubes
1 teaspoon chili powder
¼ teaspoon salt
½ cup catsup
4 ounces Cheddar cheese
12 (6-inch) frozen tortillas
1 jar taco sauce

1. Place Disc, slice side up, in Bowl. Slice lettuce; transfer to a large mixing bowl.
2. Place Blade in Bowl. Pulse to chop tomatoes, 3 to 4 seconds. Empty into a small mixing bowl. With processor running, drop garlic through the Feed Tube. Add onion. Pulse on and off to finely chop.
3. In a 10-inch skillet, sauté garlic and onion in oil.
4. Replace Blade in Bowl. Add beef cubes. Pulse on and off until finely chopped. Add beef to skillet; brown; drain off fat. Stir in chili powder salt and catsup. Reduce heat to low and keep warm.
5. Place Disc, shred side up, in Bowl; shred cheese; set aside.
6. Fry tortillas and shape into tacos as directed on package label. Place tacos on serving tray and divide ingredients among them, filling each with a layer of meat mixture, tomatoes, lettuce and cheese. Top with taco sauce.

Makes 12 servings.

Cold Stuffed Party Ham

Serve with Red and Green Cabbage Salad (see Index) and Crisp Dinner Rolls (see Index).

1 ham (10 to 12 pounds)
2 tablespoons brown sugar
1 tablespoon cider vinegar

1. Cut off ham hock. Place ham on a rack in a roasting pan. Add water to just reach the bottom of the ham; add vinegar and brown sugar. Cover and steam ham until tender enough to remove bone. Remove bone and all fat. Stuff with dressing and spread outside with dressing.
2. Cover tightly with cheese cloth and bake in a 300° F. oven for 30 minutes. Chill 24 hours. To serve, remove cheesecloth and slice very thin.

DRESSING

1 pound saltines
12 slices bread, toasted
2 medium onions, quartered
2 tablespoons sugar
1 cup ham fat

½ teaspoon dry mustard
½ cup pickle relish
4 eggs
¼ teaspoon hot pepper sauce
Dry white wine

1. Place Blade in Bowl; process crackers and bread to make fine crumbs. Process onions until finely chopped; add remaining ingredients, using enough wine to make a paste-like consistency, but not too soft.
2. Use to stuff ham.

Makes 20 servings.

Festive Ham Ring

Fill center with mashed potatoes or green peas and tiny onions. Serve Fresh Pineapple Mousse (see Index) as the grand finale.

6 slices bread in pieces
2 pounds cooked ham, cubed
2 eggs, lightly mixed
3 drops hot pepper sauce
1 teaspoon dry mustard

1 (6-ounce) can frozen orange juice
⅓ cup packed brown sugar
¼ teaspoon ground cloves

1. Place Blade in Bowl; process bread until finely crumbed. Transfer to a mixing bowl.
2. Pulse on and off to chop 1 pound of ham at a time, then run continuously to a fine grind; add to the crumbs.
3. Combine remaining ingredients in the mixing bowl. Spoon mixture into a greased 10-cup ring mold; gently pat down.
4. Bake in a preheated 350 ° F. oven 1 hour. Unmold onto a serving platter.

Makes 8 servings.

Homemade Sausage Patties

The food processor lets you make homemade sausage flavored just as you like it, but there are some important things to remember in handling pork:

1. Never taste raw or "fresh" sausage, because of the danger of trichinosis.
2. Since uncooked meat cannot be tasted to correct the seasoning, and the strength of spices is so variable, the best way to test is to mix a small batch and cook up a sample.
3. After handling new sausage, thoroughly wash your hands and any equipment or surface you have used.

Kielbasa Sausage

3 lbs pork butt or lean pork shoulder, cut into 1-inch cubes
1 pound veal, cut into 1-inch cubes

1 tablespoon marjoram
3 garlic cloves, crushed
3 teaspoons salt
1 teaspoon pepper
¼ teaspoon ground allspice

1. Place Blade in Bowl; add all ingredients and process 1 pound at a time, until coarsely chopped.
2. Transfer to a mixing bowl; shape into patties and wrap individually. (You may freeze patties until you are ready to use them.)
3. In a skillet, sauté patties over medium heat, turning to brown on both sides and cooking until well done.

Makes about 32 patties.

Country Pork Sausage

2½ pounds boneless fresh pork, cut into 1-inch cubes
½ teaspoon ginger
¼ teaspoon salt

1 teaspoon pepper
½ teaspoon poultry seasoning
¼ teaspoon cloves

1. Sprinkle meat with combined seasonings.
2. Place Blade in Bowl. Pulse on and off to chop meat, then run continuously to a fine grind.
3. To cook, form into flat patties and pan fry over moderate heat, turning until browned on both sides.

Makes about 20 patties.

Moo Shu Pork

Northern Chinese in origin, these meat-filled pancakes may be prepared in advance and frozen. Reheat before serving.

8 ounces boneless pork loin
1 garlic clove
1 small onion, halved
½ medium cabbage or bok choy,
   cut in chunks
¼ cup vegetable oil
1 tablespoon soy sauce
10 dried tiger lily buds,
   presoaked and drained

4 cloud ear mushrooms,
   presoaked and drained
3 eggs
¼ cup chicken broth
1 teaspoon salt
¼ teaspoon pepper
½ teaspoon sugar
Chinese Pancakes

1. Partially freeze pork.
2. Place Blade in Bowl; with processor running, drop garlic clove through Feed Tube and mince. Add onion; process until finely chopped. Empty onion and garlic onto waxed paper.
3. Replace Blade in Bowl; process to chop cabbage; set aside.
4. Place Disc, shred side up, in Bowl; shred pork. Pour 2 tablespoons of the oil into a wok or skillet over moderate heat, add pork and stir-fry a few minutes; add garlic, onion and soy sauce; stir-fry 30 seconds.
5. Add remaining oil; add cabbage, lillies and cloud ear and stir-fry 1 minute. Remove all ingredients and reserve.
6. Place Beater Accessory in Bowl; beat eggs slightly. Transfer to the skillet and scramble. Before the eggs set, add broth, seasonings and reserved ingredients. Stir until combined. Serve with Chinese Pancakes.

Makes filling for 8 (6-inch) pancakes.

Chinese Pancakes

1 cup boiling water
2 cups flour
Vegetable oil for frying

1. Place Blade in Bowl; add flour. With processor running, pour water through Feed Tube.
2. Remove dough to a lightly floured board; knead about 5 minutes, or until smooth and elastic.
3. Form into a 16-inch log. Cut log into 16 pieces. Roll 8 pieces into 6-inch pancakes. Lightly oil the center of these pancakes, leaving ½-inch outer rim unoiled. Roll remaining pancakes. Place an unoiled pancake on top of an oiled one and roll with a rolling pin to seal.
4. Heat vegetable oil and cook pancakes, one at a time, until lightly browned, about 2 minutes per side.
5. Make a pocket in one side of each pancake and fill with Moo Shu Pork. Serve immediately.

Makes 8 pancakes.

Pork Chops on a Bed of Apples and Cabbage

4 pork chops	1 medium onion
2 tart green apples, halved	1 tablespoon cumin
1 small head cabbage, cut to fit Feed Tube	¼ cup lemon juice
	Pepper to taste

1. In a large skillet, brown both sides of the chops in their own fat. Pour off the fat.
2. Place Disc, slice side up, in Bowl; slice apples, cabbage and onion and add to the skillet as they are sliced. Add cumin, lemon juice and pepper.
3. Cover and cook for about 20 minutes, or until chops are tender and vegetables are soft.
4. To serve, arrange chops on apple-cabbage mixture.

Makes 4 servings.

Veal Sour Cream Loaf

Noodles go very well with veal. You can make your own (see Index).

4 slices dry bread	½ pound (about 15 medium) fresh mushrooms
1½ pounds boneless veal, cut into cubes	½ cup sour cream
1 small onion, quartered	1 egg
4 carrots, peeled, cut in 1-inch pieces	1 tablespoon Worcestershire sauce

1. Place Blade in Bowl; process bread to fine crumbs and set aside.
2. Replace Blade in Bowl. Pulse on and off to chop 1 pound of meat at a time; then run continuously to a fine grind. Transfer to a mixing bowl.
3. Replace Blade in Bowl; add onion, carrots and mushrooms. Process until finely chopped. Transfer to the mixing bowl.
4. Add remaining ingredients; press into a greased 9 x 5 x 3-inch loaf pan. Bake in a preheated 350° F. oven for 1½ hours. Serve liquid from bottom of pan over slices of veal loaf.

Makes 6 servings.

Lamb Stew

Serve with fluffy rice, Red and Green Cabbage Salad (see Index) and Sour Cream Herb Bread (see Index).

2 pounds boneless lamb shoulder cut into 2-inch cubes	2 cups water
¼ cup flour	1 cup dry white wine
½ teaspoon salt	⅛ teaspoon leaf thyme
¼ teaspoon pepper	2 medium onions
2 tablespoons cooking oil	2 ribs celery, cut to fit Feed Tube
	4 medium carrots
	2 tablespoons flour

1. Mix flour with salt and pepper and coat lamb cubes.
2. Heat oil in a large saucepan and brown lamb. Add water and wine and bring to a boil. Cover, reduce heat and simmer about 30 minutes.
3. Place Disc, slice side up in Bowl. Slice onions, celery, and carrots, and add to stew. Continue cooking until lamb is tender.
4. Blend 1 cup of the liquid with flour, return it to the saucepan. Cook and stir until mixture boils. Taste and correct seasoning before serving.

Makes 6 servings.

Lamb and Cheese Pie

Begin this meal with steaming bowls of Apple Bisque (see Index).

1 pound boneless lamb, cut into cubes	4 eggs, slightly beaten
½ cup fresh parsley leaves	½ cup milk
1 small onion, quartered	1 teaspoon salt
4 ounces Cheddar cheese, cubed	¼ teaspoon pepper
	1 (8-inch) pie shell (see Index), unbaked

1. Place Blade in Bowl; pulse on and off to chop meat, then run continuously to a fine grind. Transfer to a heavy skillet and cook over low heat until browned, stirring occasionally. Drain off drippings.
2. Replace Blade in Bowl; process to chop parsley; set aside. Process to finely chop onion and empty onto a sheet of waxed paper.
3. Place Disc, shred side up, in Bowl; shred cheese and reserve ½ cup cheese. Combine remaining cheese, onion, eggs, milk, salt, and pepper with lamb. Mix well and turn into a pricked pastry shell. Sprinkle with reserved cheese and parsley over top.
4. Bake in a preheated 400° F. oven for 40 minutes or until set.

Makes 4 servings.

Moussaka

A favorite lamb and eggplant casserole from Greece. Stuffed Artichokes (see Index) would complement this dish.

1 medium eggplant, cut to
    fit Feed Tube
1 teaspoon salt
¼ cup flour
4 tablespoons olive oil
6 ounces Parmesan cheese, cubed
2 medium onions, quartered
3 tablespoons flour
6 tablespoons butter or margarine

2 pounds lamb, cubed
1 can (1 pound) tomatoes
1 can (6-ounce) tomato paste
⅛ teaspoon dried oregano
Pepper
¼ teaspoon cinnamon
1 cup dry red wine
2 cups milk

1. Place Disc, slice side up, in Bowl. Slice eggplant. Transfer slices to a mixing bowl. Sprinkle with salt and let stand 1 hour.
2. Rinse and dry slices. Dip in flour and brown on both sides in hot olive oil. Drain on paper towels.
3. Reverse Disc to shred side up in Bowl; shred cheese. Place Blade in Bowl; process to finely grate cheese; set aside. Process onions until they are finely chopped. Heat 4 tablespoons of the butter in skillet to brown onion.
4. With Blade in Bowl, pulse on and off to chop lamb 1 pound at a time; then run continuously to a fine grind.
5. Add lamb to onions in skillet; brown. Add tomatoes, tomato paste, oregano, pepper, cinnamon and wine; stir to blend. Cook slowly, uncovered, until almost all the liquid is absorbed.
6. Melt remaining butter in saucepan. Add 3 tablespoons flour and stir to blend. Stir in milk and cook and stir until mixture boils and is thickened.
7. Grease a 2½-quart casserole and arrange ½ of the eggplant slices in the bottom. Add meat mixture and cover with remaining eggplant slices. Pour sauce over all. Sprinkle with cheese. Bake in a preheated 400° F. oven 1 hour or until top is browned.

Makes 6 to 8 servings.

Chicken Casserole

Leftover chicken can be made into a delicious casserole.

2 slices dry bread, in pieces
3 cups cooked chicken meat, cut in 1-inch pieces
2 medium apples, peeled, cored and quartered
1 medium onion, quartered
2 ribs celery, cut in 1-inch pieces

8 tablespoon butter or margarine
2 tablespoons flour
1 cup heavy cream
½ cup apple cider
½ teaspoon salt
¼ teaspoon pepper
Dash grated nutmeg

1. Place Blade in Bowl; process to finely crumb bread; set aside.
2. Replace Blade in Bowl; coarsely chop chicken; set aside.
3. With Blade in Bowl, pulse on and off to finely chop apples, onions and celery; sauté in 4 tablespoons butter until they are soft. Add flour, stirring until mixture begins to thicken. Add cream, cider, salt, pepper and nutmeg. Simmer about 10 minutes, stirring constantly until the sauce is thick. Stir in the chopped chicken.
4. Pour the mixture into a buttered baking dish; sprinkle with bread crumbs and the remaining butter, melted. Bake in a 350 ° F. oven for 20 minutes or until browned.

Makes 6 servings.

Baked Mousse of Chicken

The center of this ring might be filled with Spinach Purée (see Index).

½ cup loosely packed parsley leaves
3 skinned, boneless chicken breasts, cubed
Salt and pepper to taste

¼ teaspoon nutmeg
¼ teaspoon cayenne pepper
2 cups light cream
1 egg white, lightly beaten
Sauce Aurore (see Index)

1. Place Blade in Bowl; process to finely chop parsley and reserve.
2. Chop chicken until smooth; add seasonings. Refrigerate until well chilled.
3. Replace Blade in Bowl; gradually add cream, and egg white to chicken mixture.
4. Remove to a greased 1½-quart ring mold. Cover with a buttered parchment paper (or brown bag paper) and set in a roasting pan. Pour boiling water into roasting pan until it is about 1-inch deep.
5. Bake at 400° F. for 25 to 35 minutes. Unmold. Sprinkle with chopped parsley. Serve with Sauce Aurore.

Makes 6 servings.

Chicken Croquettes

Mushroom Medley (see Index) would be fine on the side.

4 slices dry bread, in pieces
3 cups cooked chicken, cut up
1 celery rib, cut in 1-inch pieces
1 medium onion, quartered
1 cup heavy cream

Salt and pepper to taste
¼ teaspoon nutmeg
Pinch of cayenne pepper
2 tablespoons vegetable oil
2 tablespoons butter or margarine

1. Place Blade in Bowl; process bread to fine crumbs. Leave about ¼ cup of the bread crumbs in the Bowl, and empty the rest onto waxed paper.
2. Replace Blade in Bowl; process chicken, celery, and onion until finely chopped. Add cream and seasonings; blend.
3. Remove the chicken mixture to a mixing bowl; with wet hands, form croquettes and roll each of them in the bread crumbs.
4. In a large skillet, heat the oil and butter. Sauté the croquettes 3 to 4 minutes.

Makes 6 servings.

Chilled Chicken Mousse Curry

Serve with Peach Chutney (see Index).

2 envelopes unflavored gelatin
2 cups chicken broth
Juice of 1 lemon
1 teaspoon onion powder
1 teaspoon dry mustard
2 teaspoons curry powder
2 cups sour cream
2 cooked chicken breasts, cut in small pieces

3 ribs celery, cut into 1-inch pieces
½ cup blanched almonds
Lettuce
Cherry tomatoes
Shredded coconut (see Index)

1. In a medium-size mixing bowl, soften gelatin in ½ cup of the cold chicken broth. Heat remaining broth. Add heated broth to gelatin and stir until gelatin is dissolved. Add lemon juice and seasonings. Chill in refrigerator until mixture begins to thicken (about 45 minutes). Then, fold in sour cream, and mix well.
2. Place Blade in Bowl; with processor running, drop chicken pieces through Feed Tube; process to finely chop chicken. Transfer chicken to a large mixing bowl.
3. Replace Blade in Bowl; chop celery and almonds and add them to the chicken; mix well. Combine chopped chicken mixture with the gelatin and sour cream.
4. Spoon into a 1½-quart mold. Chill until firm. Unmold on a serving platter. Garnish with lettuce and cherry tomatoes. Fill center with shredded coconut.

Makes 6 servings.

Stir-Fry Chicken Lo Mein Cantonese

For a complete oriental-style meal, serve Stuffed Mushrooms (see Index) and Crumbed Ginger Pears (see Index).

2 whole chicken breasts, skinned, and boned
1 clove garlic
3 scallions, cut in 1-inch pieces
8 ounces bok choy
¼ cup vegetable oil
½ cup chicken broth
2 tablespoons soy sauce
1 tablespoon oyster sauce
½ teaspoon salt
1 teaspoon sugar
¼ teaspoon pepper
1 package (8-ounce) Chinese noodles, cooked

1. Wrap chicken breasts and place in the freezer for about an hour, until partially frozen.
2. Place Blade in Bowl. With processor running, drop garlic clove through Feed Tube; process until finely minced; mince scallions, set aside.
3. Place Disc, slice side up in Bowl. Pack bok choy into Feed Tube tightly, and press firmly on Food Pusher to make thick slices. Transfer to a mixing bowl. Slice chicken.
4. Heat 2 tablespoons of the oil in a wok or a skillet over medium heat. Add garlic and scallions; stir-fry 1 minute. Push aside. Add bok choy and stir-fry 2 minutes. Push aside. Add remaining oil if needed. Add chicken slices and stir-fry 3 minutes. Add remaining ingredients, including noodles cooked according to package directions. Stir well and combine. Heat until hot, about 2 minutes. Serve immediately.

Makes 6 servings.

Plum Duckling

1 (4 to 5 lb.) fresh or frozen
   duckling

3 apples, unpeeled, halved, cored
Plum Sauce (see following recipe)

Wash duck, pat dry. Stuff with apples. Prick skin in several places. Roast duck on rack, breast side up, in a preheated 400° F. oven for the first 30 minutes; reduce heat to 350° F. for 2 hours or until tender. Baste with Plum Sauce during last 30 minutes of baking, or until tender. Spoon remaining warm sauce over duck when it is served.

PLUM SAUCE:

1 medium onion, quartered
2 tablespoons butter or margarine,
   melted
1 can (16-ounce) pitted purple
   plums
1 can (6-ounce) frozen lemonade

¼ cup soy sauce
2 teaspoons prepared mustard
1 teaspoon ginger
1 teaspoon Worcestershire sauce
2 drops hot pepper sauce

1. Place Blade in Bowl. Chop onion. Remove to a skillet; sauté in butter or margarine until tender.
2. Replace Blade in Bowl; pureé plums with syrup. Add puréed plums and remaining ingredients to the onion in the skillet. Simmer, uncovered, for 15 minutes. This sauce may be made ahead and refrigerated or frozen.

Makes 4 servings.

Turkey Cutlets Stuffed with Veal Mousse

½ pound veal fillet, cut in 1-inch
   cubes
½ teaspoon salt
¼ teaspoon pepper
6 fresh mushrooms
1 small onion, halved
10 sprigs fresh parsley

1 egg and 1 egg white
6 ounces heavy cream
6 turkey cutlets
5 tablespoons butter or margarine
½ cup Port or Madeira wine
½ cup chicken broth
Dash of cayenne pepper

1. Trim fat from veal. Chill in refrigerator 30 minutes.
2. Place Blade in Bowl. Process meat, salt and pepper, until puréed. Remove to a mixing bowl. Replace blade and process mushrooms, onion and parsley until coarsely chopped. Add egg and egg white and blend. Stir the mixture into the veal; refrigerate for an hour.
3. Pound turkey cutlets and divide into 6 portions. Spread the mousse over each portion, and roll up each one. Tie each portion with a string. Refrigerate for 30 minutes.
4. In a large skillet, heat 4 tablespoons of the butter. Sauté the rolled cutlets, turning frequently, until golden—about 20 minutes.
5. Remove the strings; add wine and broth. Simmer, stirring in the remaining butter, until thick. Pour sauce over the portions and serve.

Makes 6 servings.

Stuffed Breast of Turkey Parmigiana

Serve this with Sweet Potato Fruit Casserole (see Index) and steamed broccoli with Hollandaise Sauce (see Index).

8 slices bread, in pieces
¼ pound Parmesan cheese, cut in 1-inch cubes
½ cup loosely packed parsley leaves
½ teaspoon marjoram
½ teaspoon thyme
1½ teaspoons salt
¼ teaspoon pepper
1 cup butter or margarine, melted
1 clove garlic, crushed
1 (3-pound) turkey breast
1 pound Kielbasa sausage (see Index)
1 (32-ounce) can Italian tomatoes
½ cup dry wine, red or white

1. Place Disc, shred side up, in Bowl; shred Parmesan cheese.
2. Place Blade in Bowl; process bread with cheese to fine crumbs. Empty crumb mixture into a large bowl, add seasonings and toss to mix well.
3. Replace Blade in Bowl; process to finely chop parsley; set aside.
4. Combine butter and garlic in a bowl. Dip turkey breast in the garlic butter, then into the crumb mixture to coat well. Stuff with sausage.
5. Bake 1 hour in a 350° F. oven, uncovered. Pour in tomatoes and wine, sprinkle with parsley and cover. Bake another 30 minutes, or until meat is tender.

Makes 6 servings.

Seafood

Gone are the days when you had to live on the seacoast to have really good fish. Modern methods of preserving and shipping have made an astonishing variety available to all of us.

Considered the food of choice for more and more people, fish is a delicious entrée for the most casual dining. But it can be served in splendor as a Turban of Salmon and Sole Mousseline, Quenelles, or Mousse of Scallops. Your food processor speedily purées raw fish for these dishes. It chops and slices vegetables and cheese to combine with fish as you prepare Salmon Zucchini Quiche or Cioppino, and many other recipes you'll find in this collection.

Shrimp Jambalaya

This Louisiana dish of Spanish origin may be made with chicken or crabmeat, but rice is essential for it to be Jambalaya.

2 cloves garlic
1 medium onion, quartered
1 green pepper, seeded and
    quartered
2 ribs celery, cut in 1-inch pieces
3 tablespoons vegetable oil
1 can (16-ounce) tomatoes
3 tablespoons tomato paste

1¼ cups water or clam juice
1 cup uncooked rice
½ teaspoon thyme
¼ teaspoon red pepper flakes
Dash of pepper
8 ounces cooked ham, cut in cubes
1½ pounds uncooked shrimp,
    shelled and deveined

1. Place Blade in Bowl; with processor running, drop garlic cloves through Feed Tube and process until finely minced. Add onion, green pepper and celery; process until finely chopped.
2. In a large skillet, sauté garlic, onion, green pepper and celery in oil until they are tender. Add tomatoes, tomato paste, water or clam juice, rice and seasonings. Cover and simmer for 25 to 30 minutes, or until rice is tender.
3. Add ham and shrimp; turn up heat and cook until shrimp is tender, about 5 minutes.

Makes 6 servings.

Scalloped Oysters

2 cups oysters, shucked, in liquid
2 slices dry bread, in pieces
6 saltines
8 tablespoons butter or margarine,
    melted

2 tablespoons oyster liquid
1 tablespoon milk
Salt and pepper to taste

1. Clean the oysters for bits of shell, and reserve liquid; set aside.
2. Place Blade in Bowl; process bread and crackers until finely ground.
3. In a shallow greased baking dish, spread a thin layer of the crumb mixture. Cover with half of the oysters, oyster liquid, milk and seasonings. Add remaining oysters and top with remaining crumbs.
4. Bake 20 minutes in a 450° F. oven.

Makes 4 servings.

Devilled Crab

This savory American dish is often served as a first course or as the main one.

4 ounces Cheddar cheese, cubed
½ green pepper, cut in 1-inch
    pieces
1 small onion, quartered
1 rib celery, cut in 1-inch lengths
2 tablespoons butter or margarine
2 tablespoons flour
1 cup milk

½ cup half and half
½ teaspoon salt
2 tablespoons catsup
1 tablespoon sherry wine
Dash cayenne pepper
2 cups hot cooked rice
12 ounces crab meat

1. Place Disc, shred side up, in Bowl. Shred cheese; set aside.
2. Place Blade in Bowl. Process green pepper, onion and celery until finely chopped; in a saucepan, sauté chopped vegetables until almost tender; blend in flour. Stir in milk, half and half and salt gradually. Cook over medium heat until smooth and thick. Add ½ cup grated cheese, catsup, sherry and cayenne; stir over low heat until cheese is melted.
3. Place ⅓ cup rice in each of 6 individual baking shells or ramekins. Stir crab into sauce mixture; spoon over rice. Sprinkle with remaining cheese. Bake in a 425° F. oven 10 to 15 minutes until bubbly.

Makes 6 servings.

Curried Lobster

Serve with bowls of coconut flakes, pine nuts, raisins, chutney and coarsely chopped cucumbers.

1 cup blanched almonds
4 tablespoons butter, or margarine,
    softened
1 small onion, quartered
1 pound cooked lobster meat,
    cut into scallops

¼ cup parsley leaves
1 tablespoon curry powder
½ cup heavy cream
Salt and pepper to taste
Cooked rice

1. Place Blade in Bowl; process almonds until finely chopped. Melt butter in a large skillet; sauté almonds.
2. Replace Blade in Bowl; process onion until finely chopped. Add to skillet and cook 3 or 4 minutes. Gently stir in lobster meat.
3. Replace Blade in Bowl; process to chop parsley and add it to the skillet along with curry powder and cream. Cook and stir until mixture boils. Season to taste.
4. Serve with rice.

Makes 6 servings.

Mousse of Scallops

Serve this to your most deserving guests with Sautéed Zucchini and Tomatoes (see Index) and Georgia Pecan Pie (see Index).

1½ pounds scallops
2 eggs
Salt and white pepper to taste
Pinch of cayenne pepper

¼ teaspoon nutmeg
2 cups heavy cream
Dilled Tomato Sauce (see Index)

1. Preheat oven to 375° F. Place Blade in Bowl; add scallops, eggs, salt, pepper, cayenne and nutmeg. With the processor running, gradually add cream through the Feed Tube. Process until thoroughly blended.
2. Spoon the mixture into a buttered 2-quart casserole or 6-inch individual ramekins and place in a large baking pan. Pour about 1½ inches boiling water in baking pan, and bake covered, 20 to 30 minutes, or until mousse is set. Serve from the casserole with Dilled Tomato Sauce.

Makes 6 servings.

Fish Dumplings (Quenelles)

Any uncooked fresh white fish (schrod, cod or halibut) may be substituted for the haddock. For added flavor and texture, peeled and chopped pistachios or sautéed chopped mushrooms may be added to the puréed fish.

Mousseline
1¼ pounds haddock
3 egg whites
1½ cups heavy cream
½ teaspoon salt
¼ teaspoon pepper

¼ teaspoon nutmeg
2 drops hot pepper sauce

Hollandaise or Aurore Sauce
  (see Index)
8 ounces Parmesan cheese

1. Place Blade in Bowl; process the fish and egg whites to purée; with the processor running, gradually pour in the cream until it is absorbed. Add seasonings and transfer the purée to a mixing bowl; cover with plastic wrap to touch the surface and refrigerate at least an hour.
2. Fill a large, somewhat shallow pot with 3 quarts lightly salted water. Bring the water to a gentle simmer. With a wet tablespoon, scoop up a small mound of the fish mixture; with a second wet tablespoon smooth and shape the mixture into an oval dumpling. Slip 4 or 5 dumplings into the water at a time, allowing 2 to 3 minutes for each batch. Cover and simmer; they will rise to float on the surface when they are done.
3. Arrange the quenelles in a buttered, oven-proof dish. Cover them with sauce.
4. Place Disc, shred side up, in Bowl; shred Parmesan cheese. Sprinkle cheese over the top of the casserole and bake in a 400° F. oven for 10 minutes. Place under the broiler for 1 or 2 minutes to brown. Serve immediately.

Makes 10 dumplings.

Turban of Salmon and Sole Mousseline

For an impressive presentation, try this mousselline wrapped in a ring of fish fillets.

Mousseline recipe (see Index)	**3 or 4 sole fillets**
3 or 4 salmon fillets	**Dill Sauce (see Index)**

1. Lay fillets, alternating salmon and sole, in a greased ring mold across the mold so they overlap slightly and the ends hang over the edges of the mold.
2. Carefully fill the mold with the chilled fish mouseline; fold the ends of the fillets over the top of it.
3. Set the mold in a roasting pan; add boiling water to come halfway up the sides of the ring.
4. Bake in a 375° F. oven for 35 to 40 minutes.
5. Remove ring mold from roasting pan; let it rest for 10 minutes. Unmold onto a serving platter.
6. Serve the turban hot with Dill Sauce or serve cold garnished with fresh dill weed.

Makes 12 to 16 servings.

Seafood Croquettes

An excellent way to use leftover cooked fish.

1 small onion, quartered	**3 slices dry bread, in pieces**
2 ribs celery, cut in 1-inch pieces	**1 egg**
¼ cup butter or margarine	**2 tablespoons water**
⅓ cup flour	**1 teaspoon dill weed**
1 cup milk	**Vegetable oil**
2 cups canned or cooked fish	**Choron Sauce (see Index)**
½ teaspoon salt	

1. Place Blade in Bowl; pulse on and off to finely chop onion and celery.
2. In a 1-quart saucepan, heat butter and sauté onion and celery until soft. Stir in flour. Add milk and cook over medium heat, stirring constantly until mixture thickens. Remove from heat; stir in fish and salt.
3. Spread mixture in a shallow dish and chill 2 hours.
4. Place Blade in Bowl; process bread to crumbs; empty onto a sheet of waxed paper.
5. Replace Blade in Bowl; add egg and water, and pulse on and off to mix. Remove Blade.
6. Divide chilled mixture into 8 parts. Wet hands and roll each piece in bread crumbs; form into round shapes. Dip in egg mixture and roll again in crumbs. Refrigerate at least 2 hours.
7. In a large heavy skillet or deep fryer, heat oil to 375° F. Fry croquettes until deep golden brown. Drain on paper towels and serve warm with Choron Sauce.

Makes 8 croquettes.

Salmon Loaf with Mushroom Sauce

A convenient dish when time is short. Fresh Tomato Soup (see Index) and Shredded Zucchini Salad (see Index) would round out the meal nicely.

14 saltines
1 small onion, halved
1 large rib celery, cut in 1-inch pieces
1 small green pepper, cut in 1-inch pieces

1 (16-ounce) can salmon, drained, bones removed
2 eggs
½ cup milk
Butter or margarine
Parsley
Mushroom Sauce (see Index)

1. Place Blade in Bowl; process crackers and vegetables together until coarsely chopped. Add salmon, eggs and milk; process until mixture is well mixed.
2. Transfer salmon mixture to a buttered loaf pan. Bake in a 350° F. oven for 30 minutes or until set in center.
3. To remove loaf from the pan, loosen edges with a knife, invert loaf onto a platter; use spatulas to turn loaf over so top is up. Garnish with parsley. Serve with Mushroom Sauce (see Index).

Makes 6 servings.

Salmon-Zucchini Quiche

The versatile zucchini gives this quiche just the needed crunch.

2½ ounces Parmesan cheese, cut in 1-inch pieces
1 small onion, halved
½ pound zucchini, cut to fit Feed Tube
4 sprigs fresh parsley
3 eggs

1 tablespoon lemon juice
¼ teaspoon dill weed
⅛ teaspoon pepper
¼ teaspoon salt
1 can (8-ounce) red salmon, drained and flaked
1 (8-inch) unbaked pie crust

1. Place Disc, shred side up, in Bowl; shred Parmesan cheese.
2. Place Blade in Bowl; process cheese until finely grated, and reserve. Process onion until finely chopped.
3. Place Disc, shred side up, in Bowl. Shred zucchini.
4. In a small saucepan, cook zucchini and onion just until tender, about 3 minutes. Drain well.
5. Place Blade in Bowl and chop parsley. Add eggs, lemon juice and seasonings; pulse on and off to mix. Add cooked zucchini and onion, cheese and salmon. Pulse on and off to mix. Pour into an 8-inch unbaked pie crust.
6. Bake 30 to 40 minutes in a 375° F. oven or until set.

Makes 1 (8-inch) pie or 6 servings.

Steamed Schrod with Fresh Tomato Dill Sauce

Schrod is young Haddock in Boston. Other species that can be handled well for steaming or poaching are carp, red snapper, sea bass and whitefish. Whole fish, thick slices, or fillets can be used.

1 pound fresh schrod

SAUCE:

2 tablespoons butter or margarine
½ red Spanish onion, quartered
½ green pepper, cut in 1-inch pieces
1 cup fresh dill leaves, tightly packed

3 ounces tomato paste
2 tablespoons flour
4 fresh tomatoes, or 1 can (16-ounce) tomatoes, drained
1 cup tomato juice

1. Place fish on a rack in a shallow pan or steamer. Pour boiling water into bottom of pan up to the level of the fish. Season water with salt, pepper, thyme and crumbled bay leaf. Cover and steam for about 10 minutes, or until fish flakes easily with a fork.
2. In a large skillet, melt butter.
3. Place Blade in Bowl; chop onion, green pepper and celery. Add to skillet and sauté. Chop dill leaves; add to the sauce along with tomato paste and flour. Chop tomatoes.
4. Stir while gradually adding tomatoes and juice. Simmer until thickened. To serve, remove schrod to a serving platter and spoon sauce over it.

Makes 4 servings.

Fried Fish and Potatoes

Needs only Cucumber and Dill Salad (see Index) and Green Chili and Cheese Cornbread (see Index) to make a meal.

¼ cup loosely packed fresh parsley leaves
3 medium onions, quartered
3 tablespoons butter or margarine
3 medium potatoes, cut to fit Feed Tube
1 pound cooked white fish, cut in pieces

2 teaspoons salt
1 teaspoon pepper
2 teaspoons Worcestershire sauce
¼ teaspoon hot pepper sauce
½ cup heavy cream
Aurore Sauce (see Index)

1. Place Blade in Bowl; process to chop parsley leaves; set aside and coarsely chop onions.
2. In a large skillet, sauté the onions in butter until soft.
3. Place Disc, shred side up, in Bowl; shred potatoes and add them to the onions. Mix well and cook over medium heat for about 5 minutes.
4. Replace Blade in Bowl; process fish until coarsely chopped. Combine the fish and seasonings with the ingredients in the skillet.
5. Flatten the mixture in the pan with a spatula. Add cream, and chopped parsley; cook until a crust forms on the bottom. Invert the skillet onto a serving platter and serve with Aurore Sauce.

Makes 6 servings.

Scandinavian Fishbake

This can be prepared up to 8 hours in advance, covered with plastic wrap or foil, and refrigerated. Coleslaw would go well with it.

2 slices dry bread, in pieces
2 tablespoons vegetable oil
¾ cup evaporated milk
1 pound perch fillets
2 tablespoons lemon juice
1 small head cauliflower, broken into buds, or 1 (10-ounce) package, frozen

1 jar (16-ounce) boiled onions, drained
4 ounces Cheddar cheese, cut in 1-inch pieces
Lemon, parsley or fresh dill

1. Place Blade in Bowl; process bread to fine crumbs. Lightly oil 9-inch baking pan. Sprinkle bottom with a dusting of crumbs. Blend remaining crumbs with evaporated milk; set aside.
2. Arrange perch, cut in serving portions, cauliflower buds and onions in baking pan. Pour crumb-milk mixture over fish and vegetables.
3. With Blade in Bowl; process cheese until finely grated and spread over the top of the ingredients. Bake in a 350° F. oven for 30 to 40 minutes. Garnish with lemon, parsley or fresh dill.

Makes 4 servings.

Baked Fillets of Bluefish

A savory mixture of flavors to enhance the bluefish.

4 medium tart apples, cored
and halved
2 medium onions
½ pound unsalted butter
or margarine

1 cup prepared mustard
2½ pounds bluefish fillets
1 cup bottled clam juice
2 cups dry white wine

1. Place Disc, slice side up, in Bowl. Pack apples in feed tube; press lightly with Food Pusher to make thin slices. Slice onions.
2. In a medium skillet, sauté apples and onions in 4 tablespoons of the butter until lightly browned. Stir in mustard.
3. Arrange fillets in a shallow baking dish. Spread mustard, apple and onion mixture evenly over the top. Pour in clam juice and about ½ cup of the wine.
4. Bake in a 350° F. oven for 5 minutes. Cover and keep fish warm while you prepare the sauce.
5. **Sauce:** Drain all the liquid from the baking dish into a medium-sized skillet. Add remaining wine and cook on high heat until the liquid in the skillet is reduced by about half. With heat turned very low, whisk in remaining butter a little at a time. As the mixture is heated the sauce will foam. Spoon over the fish and serve.

Makes 4 servings.

Baked Halibut Spanish Style

Cod, haddock or any mild-flavored fish may be substituted for halibut.
Serve with steamed rice and Chocolate Coconut Pie (see Index).

4 halibut steaks, 1 to 1½-inches
thick
3 medium tomatoes, cut to fit
Feed Tube
1 small cucumber, peeled
1 garlic clove
1 green pepper, seeded and cut
in eighths

1 medium onion, quartered
½ cup loosely packed parsley
leaves
1 bay leaf, finely crumbled
Salt to taste
Juice of 1 lemon
2 tablespoons vegetable oil

1. Put fish in an oiled baking dish. Place Disc, slice side up, in Bowl; slice tomatoes and cucumber and arrange them over the fish.
2. Replace Disc with Blade. With processor running, drop garlic clove through Feed Tube; process until finely minced. Coarsely chop green pepper and onion. Add remaining ingredients and mix.
3. Spread the mixture over the top of the fish. Bake in a 375° F. oven for about 15 minutes, or until the fish flakes easily with a fork.

Makes 4 servings.

Baked Trout Provençal

4 to 6 (½ pound each) trout
½ cup lemon juice
1 teaspoon salt
1 clove garlic
1 cup white wine
¼ cup loosely packed fresh
  parsley leaves

4 scallions, cut in 1-inch lengths
1 slice dry bread, in pieces
¼ cup butter or margarine,
  melted

1. Wipe pan-dressed trout dry. Rub with lemon juice, sprinkle with salt, set aside.
2. Place Blade in Bowl; with processor running, drop garlic clove through Feed Tube. Spread minced garlic over the bottom of a shallow, greased baking dish. Place trout, in a single layer, over the garlic. Pour wine over all.
3. Replace Blade in Bowl; process parsley, scallions and bread until finely chopped. Sprinkle over ingredients in dish and drizzle with melted butter.
4. Bake in a 400° F. oven for 20 minutes.

Makes 4 to 6 servings.

Cioppino

⅓ cup packed fresh parsley leaves
4 medium garlic cloves
2 medium green peppers, seeded
  and quartered
1 medium onion, quartered
4 medium tomatoes, cored and
  quartered
¼ cup vegetable oil
4 tablespoons butter or margarine
Pinch of saffron
Salt and pepper to taste
1 teaspoon oregano

1 teaspoon basil
2 cups dry red wine
12 littleneck clams, well scrubbed
24 mussels, well scrubbed, beards
  removed
2 pounds monkfish, cut into
  1-inch pieces, or 2 small lobster
  tails
16 ounces shrimp, shelled and
  cleaned
8 ounces scallops

1. Place Blade in Bowl; process parsley until finely chopped. Reserve for garnish. With machine running, drop garlic cloves through Feed Tube; process until minced. Pulse on and off to finely chop onion; add tomatoes and process until coarsely chopped.
2. In a large skillet, heat oil and butter. Empty ingredients from Bowl into the skillet. Stir in seasonings and wine. Remove from heat until 30 minutes before serving time.
3. Arrange clams and mussels in a single layer in a large skillet. Cover and heat about 5 to 6 minutes, until they begin to open.
4. Add monkfish or lobster in shells. Replace cover and simmer until fish flesh turns opaque, about 5 to 6 minutes.
5. Add shrimp and scallops; cover and simmer slowly about 5 minutes, or until they are white and opaque. Stir well and adjust seasonings to taste. Sprinkle with parsley.

Makes 8 servings.

Cheese, Eggs & Pasta

Cheese and eggs are a natural pair, and sometimes, as in some of the recipes that follow, are joined by pasta and vegetables. They are enjoyed in meals from morning to night, and the processor makes their preparation easier than ever.

Be sure to try the Egg, Spinach and Zucchini Tian. It can be served hot or cold, and is delicious either way. The Cheese Soufflé is especially light and gloriously golden. Homemade noodles can be yours for the making.

Invite your friends. For brunch, serve Cheese Blintzes or Country Cheese Pancakes. For a luncheon, Swiss Cheese Mousse or Gnocchi. For supper, Spanish Omelet or Ravioli. You just can't go wrong with cheese, eggs and pasta.

Cheese Blintzes

A light entrée for brunch or supper parties.

PANCAKE BATTER:

3 eggs
1 cup milk
¾ cup flour

2 tablespoons vegetable oil
½ teaspoon salt

1. Place Blade in Bowl. Add all ingredients; process until smooth. Batter sould be the consistency of heavy cream. Let batter rest for an hour or so before using.
2. Coat a 6-inch crêpe pan or skillet with a little butter and heat. Pour enough batter into pan just to coat pan. (Pour excess back into remaining batter.) Brown and turn onto paper towels, browned side up.

CHEESE FILLING:

2 cups dry Farmer cheese
2 eggs

Salt, pepper and sugar to taste
1 teaspoon vanilla extract

1. Place Blade in Bowl. Add filling ingredients; process until mixture is smooth. Put 1 tablespoon of filling on each pancake. Turn opposite sides in and roll up like a jelly roll. (If desired, blintzes may be frozen at this point.)
2. Before serving, brown blintzes well on both sides. Serve with sour cream and caviar.

Makes 10 to 12 blintzes.

Country Cheese Pancakes

Serve these for brunch with Anadama Muffins (see Index).

4 eggs
¾ cup Farmer's cheese
3 tablespoons vegetable oil
½ teaspoon vanilla extract

⅓ cup whole wheat flour
¼ teaspoon salt
1 tablespoon unprocessed bran
1 tablespoon wheat germ

1. Place Blade in Bowl; add eggs and process until foamy, 5 to 6 seconds. Add remaining ingredients and process just to blend.
2. Heat skillet or griddle until cold water bounces as it is dropped on it. Spoon ¼ cup measures of batter into pan. Turn when bubbles appear on top and the underside is light brown, about 2 to 3 minutes.
3. Serve with pats of butter and honey or maple syrup.

Makes 8 (5-inch) pancakes.

Cheese Ravioli

Serve with Pesto Sauce (see Index).

1½ cups flour
½ teaspoon salt
2 large eggs
1 tablespoon vegetable oil

1. Place Blade in Bowl; add flour and salt; process briefly to blend. With the processor running, pour the eggs and oil through the Feed Tube and process until the dough begins to form a ball; about 15 seconds. If the dough seems too sticky, add a tablespoon or two of flour. If it's too dry, add a few drops of water or part of an egg. Process again briefly.
2. Turn the dough onto a floured surface. Dough will be sticky. Dust your hands with flour and knead for 2 to 3 minutes, adding more flour if necessary until you have a smooth ball of dough.
3. Set to rest covered with a dish towel or plastic wrap for 30 minutes.
4. Divide dough into 2 pieces. Roll out two rectangular strips. Leaving a 1-inch margin around the edges, place 1 teaspoon of filling on one of the strips at 2-inch intervals. Brush water between the mounds. Lay the second pasta strip over the first. With the side of your hand, press the pasta around each mound of filling, so that the moistened strips stick together firmly.
5. Using a small sharp knife or a pastry cutter, carefully cut along and across the pasta midway between the rows of filling to separate the individual ravioli.
6. Fill a large pan ⅔ full of water, add salt and 1 tablespoon oil. Bring water to a boil, then use a skimmer to lower fresh ravioli into pan a few at a time. Cook ravioli in batches to avoid overcrowding the pan. After 3 minutes remove one ravioli and test it; it should feel tender, yet firm. If not, let the batch boil another minute.
7. When the ravioli are done, lift them with the skimmer and let excess water drain back into pan. Transfer the drained pasta to a warm serving dish. Cover dish while cooking remaining batch.

Makes 6 servings (about 60 ravioli).

CHEESE FILLING
4 ounces Parmesan cheese, cut in
   1-inch pieces
1 pound ricotta cheese
1 egg, plus 2 extra yolks
¼ teaspoon nutmeg
⅛ teaspoon salt

1. Place Blade in Bowl; process Parmesan cheese until finely grated.
2. Add ricotta cheese, egg yolks and egg, nutmeg and salt; pulse on and off until blended.

Spinach Noodles

½ (10-ounce) package frozen spinach, or 8 ounces fresh spinach, stems trimmed
2 cups flour

3 eggs
2 teaspoons olive oil
Flour

1. Cook spinach until just tender. Drain well; cool. Squeeze totally dry.
2. Place Blade in Bowl; process spinach until finely chopped. Add flour, eggs, oil and salt. Process until dough forms a ball. (Add more flour or water if necessary, so that the ball is not too sticky.) Continue processing another 15 to 20 seconds.
3. Roll dough ball in flour. Cover with plastic wrap and let stand 20 minutes.
4. Divide the dough into 4 pieces. Roll out as thinly as possible on a well-floured board. Allow the dough to dry from 15 to 30 minutes, depending on the amount of humidity in the air. The sheets of pasta may be draped over chair backs covered with kitchen towels. When dry, flour well, roll up jelly-roll fashion, and cut thin slices with a sharp knife. Unroll and separate strands. Hang up or lay flat on a floured board or cake rack.
5. To cook, drop into boiling water. Remember: homemade pasta cooks in no time at all. Dried homemade pasta takes a little longer than freshly made, but even so it will be done practically as soon as the water returns to a boil. Drain and use in noodle recipes.

Makes about 1 pound of noodles.

Cheese and Potato Casserole

With Sauteéd Zucchini and Tomatoes (see Index) and Chocolate Almond Torte (see Index) you have a great meal.

1 medium potato, peeled and halved
6 parsley sprigs
2 tablespoons butter or margarine
4 ounces Cheddar cheese, cut in 1-inch cubes

1 cup ham, cut in 1-inch cubes
1 small onion
4 eggs

1. Place Disc, slice side up, in Bowl; slice potato and onion.
2. Melt butter in a medium-sized skillet; add potato and onion slices. Sauté until tender.
3. Reverse Disc to shred side. Shred cheese. Remove and set aside.
4. Place Blade in Bowl. Add ham and parsley; chop coarsely.
5. Spoon cooked potato and onion into a greased 9 x 9 x 2-inch baking pan. Spread ham and parsley over.
6. Place Beater Accessory in Bowl. Beat eggs until light in color. Pour over casserole contents. Sprinkle shredded cheese on top.
7. Bake for 20 to 25 minutes in a 350° F. oven or until set.

Makes 4 to 6 servings.

Cheese Soufflé

For added flavor, coat the dish with grated Parmesan cheese before adding the soufflé mixture.

8 ounces Cheddar cheese,
   cubed
¼ cup butter or margarine
¼ cup flour

1 cup milk
¼ teaspoon salt
Dash of cayenne pepper
5 eggs, separated

1. Place Disc, shred side up, in Bowl; shred cheese and set aside.
2. In a medium saucepan melt butter; stir in flour until smooth. Stir in milk and seasonings until mixture thickens. Add cheese; stir until melted and remove from heat.
3. Place Beater Accessory in Bowl; beat egg yolks slightly. Gradually add cheese mixture and blend.
4. Rinse Beater Accessory and place in a clean Bowl; beat egg whites until stiff but not dry. Fold cheese sauce into egg whites.
5. Pour into a greased 2-quart soufflé dish or casserole. With tip of spoon, make an indentation around the top of the soufflé 1-inch from the edge. Bake in a preheated 350° F. oven for 45 minutes, or until golden brown. Serve immediately.

Makes 6 servings.

For individual soufflés: Pour mixture into 6 (2-cup) soufflé dishes filling ¾ full. Bake in a 350° F. oven for 30 to 35 minutes.

These soufflés may be made a day in advance and frozen. When ready to bake, place the soufflé in a cold oven. In a 300° F. oven, bake the 2-quart soufflé for 1 hour and 45 minutes; bake individual soufflés for 1 hour.

Swiss Cheese Mousse

Perfect for a summer luncheon. Hawaiian Fruit Salad (see Index) would be a good companion to this light mold.

½ small onion, halved
5 tablespoons butter or
 margarine
4 ounces Swiss cheese
½ cup flour
1½ cups milk, scalded
2 envelopes unflavored gelatin

½ cup chicken broth
4 eggs separated
¼ teaspoon Dijon mustard
¼ teaspoon salt
Pinch of nutmeg
¼ cup heavy cream
Pink Mayonnaise (see Index)

1. Place Blade in Bowl; process onion until finely chopped. In a saucepan, cook onion in 1 tablespoon of the butter until transparent.
2. Place Disc, shred side up, in Bowl; shred cheese and set aside.
3. To onion, add 4 tablespoons butter; stir in flour, and heat, stirring constantly as milk is added, until sauce is thickened and smooth. Add cheese and stir until cheese is melted. Remove from heat.
4. Soften gelatin in chicken broth Stir over low heat until gelatin is dissolved. Place Blade in Bowl. Add cheese sauce to Bowl. With processor running, add gelatin mixture through the Feed Tube; add egg yolks, mustard, salt and nutmeg; process until creamy. Cool.
5. Place Beater Accessory in Bowl; beat egg whites until stiff, but not dry. Remove.
6. In another bowl whip cream. Add whipped cream and cheese sauce to beaten egg white and gently fold together.
7. Turn mixture into a 2-quart mold rinsed with cold water. Chill for 3 hours and unmold on a serving platter. Garnish wth watercress. Serve with Pink Mayonnaise.

Makes 8 servings.

Make-ahead Party Eggs

So nice to have ready, this recipe can be varied by using different kinds of cheese, or adding chopped ham. A basket of "Love 'Em" Bran Muffins (see Index) would be very tempting.

18 or 20 slices dry bread
2½ to 3 dozen eggs
1 quart milk
Salt and pepper
1 pound Cheddar cheese, cut to fit
  Feed Tube

2 green peppers, seeded and halved
2 medium onions
½ pound fresh mushrooms
½ cup butter or margarine

1. Place Blade in Bowl. Crumb enough bread to spread bread crumbs over 3 generously buttered 13 x 9 x 2-inch baking pans.
2. Mix eggs and milk in 2 batches, transferring mixture to a large mixing bowl as it is mixed. Add salt and pepper to taste.
3. Place Disc, shred side up, in Bowl; shred cheese and add it to the egg mixture.
4. Reverse Disc to slice side up; slice the peppers, onions and mushrooms. Sauté them several minutes in butter; cool and add them to the mixture. Mix lightly and pour over the bread crumbs in the pans. Each pan should be about ¾ full. You may need to add more beaten eggs and milk.
5. Chill overnight. Bake in a 350° F. oven for 30 minutes, or until center is firm.

Makes about 25 to 30 servings.

Egg, Spinach and Zucchini Tian

This is equally good if served chilled.

2 (10-ounce) packages fresh
  spinach, washed and stems
  removed
8 ounces Parmesan cheese
½ cup fresh parsley leaves
1 or 2 garlic cloves

2 medium onions
3 medium zucchini, ends trimmed
¼ cup butter or margarine
Salt and pepper to taste
1 cup milk
4 eggs

1. Cook spinach in water that clings to leaves, heating just until wilted; drain spinach.
2. Place Disc, slice side up, in Bowl. Shred Parmesan cheese; until finely grated; set aside. Chop parsley; set aside.
3. Place Blade in Bowl; with processor running, drop garlic cloves through Feed Tube.
4. Remove Blade and place Disc, slice side up, in Bowl; slice onions and zucchini.
5. In a large skillet, melt butter, add zucchini, onion and garlic. Cook to soften but not brown. Add spinach and toss together. Add parsley and seasonings. Place in a buttered, shallow, 2-quart casserole.
6. Place Beater Accessory in Bowl; beat milk and eggs lightly; pour over vegetables. Sprinkle with cheese.
7. Bake in a 375° F. oven for 30 minutes or until cheese bubbles and eggs are set in center.

Makes 6 servings.

Gnocchi

Puffs of light, tender pasta filled with spinach and ricotta.

4 ounces Parmesan cheese	2 tablespoons butter or margarine
1 pound fresh spinach, washed and stems removed	1 pound ricotta cheese
1 tablespoon chopped fresh parsley	2 cups flour
1 garlic clove	1 teaspoon salt
	3 eggs
	½ cup butter or margarine, melted

1. Place Disc in Bowl, shred side up; shred Parmesan cheese. Place Blade in Bowl; grate Parmesan and set aside.
2. Place Blade in Bowl; chop spinach, parsley and garlic; sauté in butter until soft and the liquid from the spinach has evaporated. Set aside to cool.
3. Mix together the cheese, half the flour, the spinach mixture and salt. Add the eggs and work the mixture well, adding more flour gradually until you have a firm but malleable dough. Divide the mixture into 12 to 15 pieces; form each piece into thick, short sausage shapes.
4. Roll the gnocchi lightly in the remaining flour. Drop them carefully into a large pot of very gently simmering water. Don't let the water boil or the action may cause the gnocchi to disintegrate. When the gnocchi rise to the surface of the water they are finished cooking.
5. Remove them with a skimmer, drain well and place them in an oven-proof baking dish lightly coated with butter. Pour the melted butter over them; sprinkle with grated Parmesan cheese and bake in a 350° F. oven for 20 to 25 minutes.

Makes 6 servings.

Pineapple Noodle Pudding

½ pound medium egg noodles	4 tablespoons butter or margarine
Salt	½ cup packed brown sugar
6 graham crackers	3 eggs
1 teaspoon cinnamon	1 cup sour cream
3 tablespoon sugar	1 teaspoon vanilla extract
1 small pineapple, peeled and cut in 1-inch pieces	⅓ cup seedless raisins
8 ounces cottage cheese	

1. Cook noodles in boiling water and salt about 5 minutes; drain, rinse in cold water.
2. Place Blade in Bowl; process graham crackers, cinnamon and sugar until finely crumbed, set aside.
3. Replace Blade in Bowl, process pineapple until coarsely chopped; transfer to a large mixing bowl.
4. Replace Blade in Bowl; add cottage cheese, butter, brown sugar, eggs, sour cream and vanilla. Blend well and add to the pineapple.
5. Add noodles and raisins to the mixing bowl; toss to mix well.
6. Pour mixture into a greased 3-quart casserole or a 13 x 9-inch baking pan; bake in a preheated 350° F. oven for 1 hour.

Makes 10 to 12 servings.

Vegetables

Your food processor is a blessing when preparing vegetables. It saves your hands as well as time. It chops onions as fine as you like (without tears), makes thin, even slices of potatoes or zucchini, or French-cuts them, if you prefer. It grates potatoes for Potato Pancakes with not a scratch on your fingers. It smoothly purées for soufflés—all in a matter of minutes.

When shopping for vegetables, select them with the size of the Feed Tube in mind. Try to find those that are long and narrow and need little trimming. For best flavor, use only those fresh vegetables that are firm and ripe; otherwise it's better to buy them canned or frozen.

Stuffed Artichokes

Artichokes are shaped for stuffing. Use ½ cup less bread crumbs and add ½ cup finely chopped shrimp or ham, if you wish.

4 artichokes
3 slices dry bread, in pieces
1 clove garlic
1 medium onion, quartered
½ cup fresh chives, snipped
1 cup fresh parsley leaves, loosely packed

4 ounces Cheddar cheese
1 pound butter or margarine, melted
¼ cup water or chicken broth
1 tablespoon olive oil

1. Remove stems and about ½ inch from tips of leaves of the artichokes.
2. Cook covered with water in a large pot for about 30 minutes, or until stem pierces easily with a fork. Drain and cool.
3. Remove thistle-like choke from the center of each artichoke with a spoon or paring knife. Place artichokes, flat side down, in a casserole.
4. Place Blade in Bowl; process bread to fine crumbs. Remove to a mixing bowl; set aside. With processor running, process garlic clove until finely minced; add onion, chives, and parsley and process until finely chopped. Mix with bread crumbs.
5. Place Disc, shred side up, in Bowl; shred cheese and add to the bread crumb mixture. Stir in butter.
6. Press stuffing down between the leaves of the artichokes and across the top. Tie a string around each artichoke to hold it together. Pour in water or broth, and sprinkle olive oil over the tops.
7. Cover and bake in a 350° F. oven for about 1 hour.

Makes 4 servings.

Pickled Beets

A savory vegetable that adds zest and color. Try it with Fish Dumplings (see Index).

6 or 7 fresh beets, cooked and peeled; reserve cooking liquid
2 medium onions, halved
1 cup beet cooking liquid (or chicken broth)

½ cup cider vinegar
½ teaspoon peppercorns
1 bay leaf, crumbled
¼ cup sugar
Salt to taste

1. Place Disc, slice side up, in Bowl; slice onions; remove to a saucepan with beet cooking liquid. Add vinegar and seasonings and mix.
2. Replace Disc in Bowl; slice beets and add to saucepan. Bring to a boil. Serve hot or cold.

Makes 6 servings.

Butternut Squash Soufflé

¾ **pound butternut squash,**
  peeled and cut into small
  pieces
4 tablespoons butter or margarine

Salt and pepper to taste
½ **teaspoon nutmeg**
5 eggs, separated

1. Cook the squash until tender. Place Blade in Bowl: purée the squash, add butter, seasonings and egg yolks and blend.
2. Place Beater Accessory in a clean Bowl; beat the egg whites until stiff, but not dry; fold into the squash mixture.
3. Pour into a buttered 1½-quart soufflé dish and bake in a 350° F. oven for 45 minutes, or until brown.

Makes 6 servings.

VARIATIONS:

Spinach: use 1 cup blanched and chopped spinach.

Broccoli: use 1 cup cooked and puréed broccolli and ¼ cup grated Parmesan cheese.

Carrot: use 1 cup cooked and puréed carrots.

Braised Red Cabbage and Apples

This is especially good with pork or poultry.

1 (2 to 3 pound) head red
  cabbage, cut to fit Feed
  Tube
2 medium onions,
  quartered
2 medium apples, unpeeled
  and quartered
½ **cup butter or margarine**

1 cup currant jelly
¼ **cup brown sugar**
⅓ **cup red wine vinegar**
Salt and pepper to taste
1 teaspoon mustard seeds
2 tablespoons caraway
  seeds

1. Place Disc, slice side up, in Bowl; process to finely slice cabbage. Soak in cold salted water 20 minutes.
2. Place Blade in Bowl; process onions and apples until finely chopped.
3. Melt butter in a large skillet, add drained cabbage; sauté until tender, about 5 minutes. Add onions, apples and remaining ingredients. Simmer 6 to 8 minutes.

Makes 4 servings.

Orange Carrots

1 pound carrots, cut to fit Feed
   Tube
¾ cup water
¼ teaspoon salt
2 strips orange peel

1 medium orange, peeled and
   seeded
6 or 8 chives
2 tablespoons butter or
   margarine

1. Place Disc, slice side up, in Bowl; slice carrots. Cook sliced carrots in salted water, covered, about 5 minutes, or until just tender. Drain.
2. Place Blade in Bowl; with processor running, drop orange peel through Feed Tube to grate, add orange sections and chives and process until finely chopped.
3. Add orange, grated peel, butter and chives to carrots in the saucepan. Add butter. Heat and stir over low heat until butter is melted.

Makes 4 servings.

Sweet and Sour Carrots

1 pound fresh carrots, cut to fit
   Feed Tube
1 can (8-ounce) pineapple chunks,
   drained, syrup reserved
1 green pepper, quartered and
   seeded

1 small onion
1 tablespoon cornstarch
1 tablespoon soy sauce
1 tablespoon vinegar

1. Place Disc, slice side up, in Bowl. Slice carrots. Transfer to a skillet.
2. Pour pineapple juice over carrots; cover and simmer 8 to 10 minutes until they are just tender.
3. Place Blade in Bowl; process the pepper and onion until coarsely chopped. Add to the skillet.
4. In a small mixing bowl, blend the cornstarch, soy sauce and vinegar together. Combine with the pineapple chunks, and add to ingredients in the skillet. Stir, and cook until sauce is thickened and shiny.

Makes 4 to 6 servings.

Sautéed Celery with Hollandaise Sauce

1 stalk celery, ribs cut to fit Feed
   Tube
1 medium onion, halved
2 tablespoons butter or margarine

Salt and pepper to taste
Hollandaise Sauce (see Index)
¼ cup chopped pimiento

1. Place Disc, slice side up, in Bowl. Pack celery in Feed Tube tightly and vertically, alternating the fat and thin ends. Press lightly on Food Pusher to make thin slices; slice onion.
2. Heat the butter in a skillet; add celery, onion and seasonings. Cook over medium heat about 5 minutes until celery is tender.
3. To serve, spoon sauce over sautéed celery and sprinkle with chopped pimiento.

Makes 4 to 6 servings.

Iowa Corn Pie

Practically a meal in itself. A tossed green salad and Apple Bread Pudding (see Index) is all you need add.

35 saltines
½ cup melted butter or margarine
1 small onion, halved
2 eggs
1¼ cups milk

2 cups corn kernels
¼ teaspoon salt
Dash white pepper
2 tablespoons flour
Paprika

1. Place Blade in Bowl; process to finely chop crackers. Transfer to a mixing bowl; combine crumbs with melted butter. Set aside about half a cup of the mixture. Press remainder into 9-inch pie plate, using a spoon.
2. Process onion until finely chopped; add eggs and process to mix.
3. In a 2-quart saucepan, mix 1 cup of the milk, corn kernels, salt, pepper and flour. Heat and stir until mixture comes to a boil and thickens, then reduce heat and simmer for several minutes. Blend in remaining milk. Cool slightly. Gradually add eggs-onion mixture, stirring well.
4. Pour into the prepared pie shell and sprinkle with reserved crumbs and paprika. Bake in a 350° F. oven for 15 minutes. Cut and serve hot.

Makes 8 servings.

Eggplant Casserole

This versatile vegetable can be fixed a number of ways. The processor makes quick work of preparation for this casserole.

4 ounces Parmesan cheese
2 slices dry bread, in pieces
2 garlic cloves
1 medium eggplant, cut to fit Feed Tube
4 medium tomatoes, halved

2 green peppers, seeded and halved
6 tablespoons butter or margarine, melted
Salt and pepper
Olive oil

1. Place Disc, shred side up, in Bowl; shred cheese. Place Blade in Bowl; process to finely grated cheese, and crumb bread. Remove to a mixing bowl; mix with 2 tablespoons of the butter. With processor running, drop garlic cloves through Feed Tube; process until finely minced.
2. Place Disc, slice side up, in Bowl; slice eggplant and empty into a buttered 2-quart casserole. Slice tomatoes and peppers. Arrange over eggplant slices; season to taste and spread cheese and crumbs over the top. Sprinkle with a few drops of olive oil.
3. Bake in a 350° F. oven for 30 minutes, or until eggplant is just tender.

Makes 6 servings.

Mushroom Medley

Mushrooms have many fine attributes; they are always available, have a good taste and texture, are ready to use with the wipe of a damp cloth, and are readily combined with whatever other vegetables you have on hand, as in the following...

1 pound fresh mushrooms
4 ribs celery, cut into 1-inch pieces
1 medium onion
1 green pepper, seeded, halved

1 red pepper, seeded, halved
5 tablespoons butter or margarine
2 tablespoons vegetable oil
Salt and pepper to taste

1. Place Disc, slice side up, in Bowl. Slice mushrooms, celery, onion and peppers.
2. Heat butter and oil in a large skillet. Sauté vegetables, stirring frequently, for about 5 minutes, or until they are tender. Add seasonings.

Makes 6 servings.

Au Gratin Potatoes

6 medium baking potatoes, peeled and cut to fit Feed Tube
8 ounces Cheddar cheese
½ teaspoon salt

½ teaspoon pepper
Paprika
4 tablespoons butter or margarine

1. Place Disc, slice side up, in Bowl; process to thinly slice potatoes. Arrange slices in a well-buttered baking dish.
2. Reverse Disc to shred side up; shred cheese. Spread over potato slices. Sprinkle with salt, pepper and paprika. Dot with butter.
3. Bake in a 350° F. oven for 1 hour, or until potatoes are soft.

Makes 6 servings.

French Fried Potatoes

The processor quickly cuts potatoes for frying, making it easy to serve them freshly fried.

**6 medium white or sweet potatoes,
  peeled and cut to fit Feed Tube**
Vegetable oil or shortening
Salt

1. Place French Fry Disc in Bowl. French-cut potatoes. Dry well; deep-fry in about 2 inches of cooking oil 400° F. Fry 5 to 6 minutes, or until golden.
2. Use a slotted spoon to remove potatoes; drain on paper toweling. Season to taste.

Makes 6 servings.

Potato Pancakes (Latkes)

A traditional Channukah party dish in many Jewish households.

1 medium onion, quartered
3 eggs
**3 medium potatoes, cut to fit
  Feed Tube**
2 tablespoons flour

1 teaspoon lemon juice
Salt to taste
½ teaspoon pepper
2 tablespoons vegetable oil

1. Place Blade in Bowl; process onion until finely chopped.
2. Place Beater Accessory in Bowl; add eggs and beat.
3. Place Disc, shred side up, in bowl; shred potatoes.
4. Replace Blade in Bowl; add flour, lemon juice, salt and pepper. Process to blend well.
5. Heat oil in a large skillet; spoon 2 heaping tablespoonfuls of potato mixture into skillet for each pancake. Brown on both sides. Serve with applesauce, or sour cream, if you prefer.

Makes 12 pancakes.

Spinach Tomato Quiche

Spinach is delicious by itself or combined with foods as it is in the following recipe.

10 ounces fresh spinach, stemmed
6 ounces Swiss cheese, cut to fit
  Feed Tube
2 medium tomatoes, quartered
4 scallions, cut in 1-inch pieces
3 eggs
1 teaspoon basil

¾ cup milk
½ teaspoon salt
¼ teaspoon pepper
1 garlic clove
1 unbaked 9-inch pie shell
  (see Index)

1. Rinse and cook spinach in the water left on the leaves, about 5 minutes. Drain and cool.
2. Place Disc, shred side up, in Bowl; shred cheese; set aside.
3. Remove Disc. Place Blade in Bowl; process tomatoes and scallions, pulsing on and off until tomatoes are coarsely chopped. In a small saucepan, cook tomatoes and scallions a few minutes.
4. Combine spinach with remaining ingredients in Bowl. Pulse on and off until spinach is coarsely chopped and mixture is blended.
5. Spread shredded cheese in the bottom of the pie shell. Pour spinach mixture over cheese. Spoon cooked tomato-onion mixture around the edge of the quiche. Bake in a 450° F. oven for 15 minutes, then reduce heat to 350° F. Bake 20 minutes longer or until top is golden brown and set. Let quiche stand 10 minutes before serving. Cut in wedges to serve.

Makes 8 servings.

Spinach Purée

Serve as a side dish, or a marvelous omelet filling.

2 slices dry bread, in pieces
8 tablespoons butter or
  margarine
2 packages (10-ounce each) fresh
  spinach, coarse stems trimmed
½ teaspoon salt

¼ teaspoon pepper
1 teaspoon lemon juice or
  vinegar
2 tablespoons light cream
¼ teaspoon nutmeg

1. Place Blade in Bowl; process bread until finely crumbed.
2. In a medium skillet brown crumbs in 4 tablespoons of the butter; set aside.
3. Cook spinach for about 5 minutes in the water left on the leaves after they have been rinsed; drain and cool.
4. Place Blade in Bowl. Add spinach, remaining melted butter, salt, pepper, lemon juice or vinegar, cream and nutmeg. Process with on and off pulses until puréed. Serve immediately, topped with buttered bread crumbs.

Makes 4 servings.

Sweet Potato Fruit Casserole

A favorite accompaniment to poultry and pork.

3 medium apples, quartered
1½ cups fresh cranberries
⅓ cup packed brown sugar
8 medium sweet potatoes, cooked,
  peeled and quartered

¼ cup butter or margarine
½ teaspoon cinnamon
½ teaspoon mace
⅓ cup heavy cream
Butter or margarine

1. Place Blade in Bowl; process apples, cranberries and brown sugar until fruit is coarsely chopped and set aside.
2. Replace Blade in Bowl; purée sweet potatoes. Add butter, cinnamon, mace and cream; process to blend.
3. Spread a layer of sweet potato purée over the bottom of a greased 2½-quart casserole. Layer chopped fruit and potatoes, dot with butter.
4. Bake in a 350° F. oven for 35 to 40 minutes, or until browned and bubbly.

Makes 10 servings.

Escalloped Tomatoes

1 slice dry bread, in pieces
1 small onion, quartered
4 tablespoons butter or margarine
¾ teaspoon basil

¼ teaspoon salt
⅛ teaspoon pepper
4 medium tomatoes, cut to fit
  Feed Tube

1. Place Blade in Bowl; process bread to fine crumbs and set aside. Process onion until finely chopped.
2. In a saucepan, melt butter over moderate heat. Add onion and cook until translucent. Remove from heat and stir in bread crumbs, basil, salt and pepper.
3. Place Disc in Bowl; slice tomatoes. Arrange a layer of tomato slices in a buttered 1½-quart casserole; sprinkle with a third of the bread crumb mixture. Repeat layers twice, ending with bread crumbs. Bake in a 350° F. oven for 30 minutes.

Makes 4 servings.

Cantonese Vegetable Stir-fry

1 large onion, cut to fit Feed Tube
3 ribs celery, cut to fit Feed Tube
2 medium carrots
2 scallions, cut in 1-inch pieces
2 tablespoons vegetable oil
2 chicken bouillon cubes
1 cup hot water

4 ounces broccoli buds
6 ounces pea pods, fresh or frozen
1½ tablespoons cornstarch
2 tablespoons soy sauce
¼ teaspoon ginger
1½ cups cooked rice

1. Place Disc, slice side up in Bowl; slice onion, celery and carrots; transfer to a mixing bowl.
2. Place Blade in Bowl; chop scallions.
3. Heat oil in a large skillet or wok; stir-fry prepared vegetables for about 5 minutes.
4. Dissolve chicken bouillon in hot water and add to vegetables.
5. Add broccoli buds and pea pods.
6. Mix cornstarch, soy sauce and ginger; stir into vegetables. Bring to a boil.
7. Serve at once over rice.

Makes 6 servings.

Sautéed Zucchini and Tomatoes

3 medium zucchini, ends
 trimmed
4 tablespoons butter or margarine

3 medium tomatoes, halved
Salt and pepper to taste

1. Place Disc, slice side up, in Bowl; process to thinly slice zucchini. Empty into a large skillet. Add butter and sauté 4 to 5 minutes.
2. Place Blade in Bowl; add tomatoes and pulse on and off just until coarsely chopped. Add to the skillet along with seasonings. Cook and stir until heated through. Serve immediately.

Makes 6 servings.

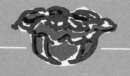 

Salads & Sandwiches

Salads have a carefree connotation ("my salad days"), and they do complement a meal happily. In California, a green salad is often served as an appetizer, but in most of the country, salads accompany the main course. We have coleslaws, enjoying a revival with the advent of the food processor, fruit salads and an impressive Avocado Mousse (see Index) that looks so fantastic on a buffet table (and can be made well before the guests arrive). Come to think about it, salads are one of the few things that's fun and good for you, too!

Your food processor excels when used to combine foods for salads or sandwich fillings. Take advantage of its assistance and vary the dressings and spreads. You could serve a different salad or sandwich for days before you began to repeat.

Apple Salad

1 cup walnuts
1 rib celery, cut in 1-inch pieces
2 medium tart apples, peeled
   and cored
1 medium apple, unpeeled
   and cored

½ cup mayonnaise
1 ½ teaspoons sugar
¼ teaspoon celery seed
Lettuce leaves

1. Place Blade in Bowl; process walnuts and celery until coarsely chopped. Add apples and pulse on and off just to chop.
2. Empty into a mixing bowl; add mayonnaise, sugar and celery seed. Toss to blend ingredients.
3. Serve in a large, lettuce-lined bowl, or on individual lettuce-lined plates.

Makes 4 to 6 servings.

Avocado Mousse

An airy, attractive molded salad; ideal for any buffet table.

1 envelope unflavored gelatin
¾ cup cold water
½ cup horseradish root, cut in
   1-inch pieces
3 medium avocados, peeled, pitted,
   and cut in pieces

3 tablespoons lemon or lime juice
½ teaspoon sugar
¼ teaspoon salt (optional)
⅛ teaspoon white pepper
½ pint heavy cream
Watercress sprigs

1. Sprinkle gelatin over ¼ cup water. Stir over low heat until gelatin is dissolved. Remove from heat, add remaining water; set aside.
2. Place Blade in Bowl. Chop horseradish root until finely chopped. Process avocado with on and off pulses just until smooth. While processor is running, add sugar, seasonings and cooled gelatin through Feed Tube.
3. Transfer mixture to a mixing bowl; chill until it is slightly thickened.
4. Place Beater Accessory in Bowl; whip cream. Gently fold whipped cream into avocado mixture and spoon into a lightly oiled 1½-quart ring mold. Chill until firm. Unmold and serve garnished with watercress.

Makes 6 servings.

Molded Cranberry Salad

A pretty salad to grace your holiday table.

1½ cups fresh cranberries
½ cup whole almonds
1 package (3-ounce) raspberry
   gelatin

¼ teaspoon nutmeg
1 cup boiling water
1 cup pineapple juice
3 ribs celery, cut to fit Feed Tube

1. Place Blade in Bowl. Chop cranberries and almonds. In a mixing bowl, mix the raspberry gelatin and nutmeg together. Add boiling water. Stir until dissolved. Add pineapple juice. Combine with cranberries and almonds. Chill until thickened.
2. Place Disc, slice side up, in Bowl; slice celery. Stir celery into mixture. Pour into a 5-cup mold or individual molds. Chill until firm. Unmold to serve.

Makes 8 to 10 servings.

Cucumber and Dill Salad

Goes especially well with salmon.

4 medium cucumbers, peeled
½ cup fresh dill, loosely packed
¼ cup white vinegar

1 tablespoon sugar
Salt to taste
Lettuce leaves

1. Place Disc, slice side up, in Bowl. Process to thinly slice cucumbers. Transfer slices to a mixing bowl.
2. Place Blade in Bowl. Chop dill. Add to mixing bowl with vinegar, sugar and salt. Toss to blend. Cover and refrigerate. Serve on lettuce leaves.

Makes 4 servings.

Coleslaw

The processor makes shredding cabbage so simple, anyone can make coleslaw.

4 ribs celery, cut into
   1-inch pieces
1 small head cabbage, cored and
   cut to fit Feed Tube
6 radishes

1 tablespoon caraway seeds
½ cup Aioli Sauce (see Index)
2 teaspoons cider vinegar
1 tablespoon lemon juice
1 tablespoon brown sugar

1. Place Disc, slice side up, in Bowl; Slice celery and cabbage, using light pressure on the Food Pusher.
2. Reverse Disc to shred side. Stack radishes in Feed Tube and shred. Remove vegetables to a large bowl.
3. Place Blade in Bowl. Process Aioli Sauce with vinegar, lemon juice and brown sugar. Pour over cabbage mixture. Toss to blend. Cover and refrigerate.

Makes 8 servings.

Red and Green Cabbage Salad

Let nature's colors brighten your table.

¼ medium head red cabbage, cut to fit Feed Tube
½ medium head green cabbage, cut to fit Feed Tube
1 egg yolk
½ teaspoon salt
½ teaspoon prepared mustard
Dash of cayenne pepper
2 tablespoons cider vinegar
¾ cup evaporated milk
Red lettuce leaves

1. Place Disc, slice side up, in Bowl; slice cabbages separately. Remove to separate bowls.
2. Place Blade in Bowl. Process egg yolk, salt, mustard, pepper and vinegar. Gradually add milk while motor is running. Pour half of dressing on cabbage of each color and mix lightly.
3. Cover bowls and refrigerate. To serve, put some red cabbage salad on each lettuce leaf and top with green cabbage salad.

Makes 4 servings.

Hawaiian Fruit Salad

A tropical delight

1 small fresh pineapple, peeled and cut to fit Feed Tube
8 medium carrots
½ fresh coconut, cut to fit Feed Tube
½ cup raisins
⅓ cup mayonnaise or salad dressing
2 teaspoons lemon juice

1. Place Disc, shred side up, in Bowl; shred pineapple. Empty into a mixing bowl.
2. Shred carrots and coconut.
3. Add shredded carrots, coconut, raisins, mayonnaise, and lemon juice to pineapple. Toss lightly. Cover and chill until ready to serve.

Makes 6 to 8 servings.

Layered Fruit Salad with Walnut Dressing

A delightful combination of flavors and textures.

1 head iceberg lettuce, cut to fit
   Feed Tube
1 cup raisins or pitted dates
6 seedless oranges, peeled and
   sectioned
1 pound seedless grapes

1 cup walnuts
6 tablespoons vegetable oil
4 tablespoons lemon juice
1 teaspoon marjoram
Salt and pepper to taste

1. Place Disc, slice side up, in Bowl; slice lettuce and spread in bottom of a glass serving bowl.
2. Place Blade in Bowl; process to finely chop raisins or dates; spread over sliced lettuce.
3. Add a layer of orange sections and grapes.
4. Replace Blade in Bowl; process to coarsely chop walnuts; add oil, lemon juice, and seasonings; blend and pour over salad. Cover serving dish with plastic wrap and refrigerate.
5. Toss before serving.

Makes 6 servings.

Marinated Mushroom Salad

This salad can give a little zip to a meal wherever it is needed. Serve it as an appetizer, as part of an antipasto platter, or as a side dish.

1 pound fresh mushrooms
2 cloves garlic
1 medium onion, quartered
½ cup fresh parsley leaves

¾ cup red wine vinegar
¾ cup vegetable oil
Lettuce leaves
Watercress sprigs

1. Place Disc, slice side up, in Bowl. Slice mushrooms, remove them to a glass bowl.
2. Place Blade in Bowl; with processor running, drop garlic cloves through Feed Tube and process until finely minced. Add onion, parsley and remaining ingredients except lettuce and watercress. Pulse on and off to coarsely chop onion and parsley.
3. Pour marinade over sliced mushrooms. Cover and refrigerate several hours, stirring occasionally.
4. To serve, remove mushrooms from marinade with a slotted spoon; mound on lettuce leaves and watercress on a large platter or individual salad bowls. Serve remaining marinade separately.

Makes 10 to 12 servings.

Hot Potato Salad

A main dish salad. Serve this with Fresh Vegetable Soup (see Index) and Pumpkin Nut Pie (see Index) to complete the meal.

4 large potatoes, cut to fit
   Feed Tube
1 large onion, cut in half
2 tablespoons butter or margarine
3 eggs
½ cup sugar
¼ cup cider vinegar

2 tablespoons flour
Dash salt
¼ cup cold water
1 cup hot water
3 ribs celery, cut in 1-inch pieces
6 hard-cooked eggs, halved
Celery seed

1. Place French Fry Disc in Bowl. Slice potatoes and onion. Sauté potatoes and onion about 5 minutes in butter.
2. In a saucepan, combine eggs, sugar, vinegar, flour, salt and cold water. Stir and add hot water. Cook on low heat until mixture thickens.
3. Place Blade in Bowl; process celery and hard-cooked eggs until coarsely chopped. Toss together with cooked potatoes and onions. When ready to serve, pour hot dressing over potato mixture, and sprinkle with celery seed.

Makes 8 to 10 servings.

Shredded Zucchini Salad

A crisp and crunchy salad to serve with a soft entrée such as Cheese Soufflé (see Index).

1 pound zucchini, ends trimmed
1 small red onion
1 clove garlic
¼ cup fresh parsley leaves
⅓ cup wine vinegar

¼ cup vegetable oil
½ teaspoon fennel seed, crushed
Salt and pepper to taste
1 head romaine lettuce in bite-size
   pieces

1. Place Disc, shred side up, in Bowl; shred zucchini. Transfer to a large bowl.
2. Place Blade in Bowl; with processor running, process onion, garlic and parsley until finely chopped. Add to the mixing bowl.
3. Place Blade in Bowl; add vinegar, oil, fennel seed, salt and pepper. Pour over zucchini and toss. Chill; toss again to blend flavors and serve over lettuce leaves.

Makes 4 to 6 servings.

Mayonnaise

1 egg
1 teaspoon salt
1 teaspoon dry mustard

2 tablespoons lemon juice or
vinegar
1 cup vegetable oil

1. Place Blade in Bowl. Process egg, salt, mustard, lemon juice, and 1
   tablespoon of the oil a few seconds. While processor is running, add
   remaining oil through Feed Tube in a slow stream. After all oil is added,
   process about 15 seconds more.
2. Store in a covered container in the refrigerator 3 to 5 days.

Makes about 1 cup.

VARIATIONS:

Green Goddess: Add 3 fillets of anchovies, 1 scallion, ¼ cup parsley leaves,
1 teaspoon tarragon, and 2 tablespoons chives.

Pink: Add Dijon mustard and 1 tablespoon tomato paste or catsup.

For fruit salads: Add 1½ teaspoons curry powder and ½ cup chopped
coconut.

For vegetable salads: Add 1 tablespoon finely chopped onion or carrot.

Yogurt Vegetable Dressing

2 scallions, cut in pieces
½ green pepper, cut in 1-inch
   pieces
½ red pepper, cut in 1-inch pieces
1 rib celery, cut in 1-inch pieces

3 tablespoons vegetable oil
½ teaspoon salt
¼ teaspoon pepper
1 teaspoon white vinegar
1 cup plain yogurt

1. Place Blade in Bowl. Process scallions, peppers and celery until finely
   chopped. Add remaining ingredients, and process just until blended.
2. Chill well for several hours.

Makes about 1½ cups.

Thousand Island Dressing

1 hard-cooked egg, halved
3 small sweet gherkins
3 pimiento strips

1 cup mayonnaise
½ cup catsup

1. Place Blade in Bowl. Process egg, gherkins, pimiento until finely chopped. Add remaining ingredients, and process until blended.
2. Store in a covered container in the refrigerator 3 to 5 days.

Makes about 1½ cups.

Creamy Roquefort Dressing

1 cup vegetable oil
⅓ cup cider vinegar
2 cloves garlic
1 teaspoon dry mustard

1 teaspoon Worcestershire sauce
½ cup mayonnaise
4 ounces Roquefort cheese
Pepper to taste

1. Place Blade in Bowl. Add all ingredients and process several seconds until blended.
2. Store in a covered container in the refrigerator 3 to 5 days.

Makes 1¾ cups.

Chicken Salad Sandwiches

2 cups cold cooked chicken, cubed
1 rib celery, cut in 1-inch pieces
1 small tomato, quartered
1 small onion, quartered
1 sweet pickle, quartered

¼ cup mayonnaise
Salt and pepper to taste
Dash of rosemary
8 slices bread or 4 rolls

1. Place Blade in Bowl. Add chicken, vegetables, pickle and seasonings. Process until mixture is blended. Adjust seasonings to taste.
2. Spread filling on each of 4 slices of bread. Make into sandwiches. Cut in half. Serve with pickles or cherry tomatoes.

Makes 4 sandwiches.

Tuna Salad Sandwiches

Probably the all-time favorite sandwich.

2 scallions, cut in 1-inch lengths
2 ribs celery, cut in pieces
1 small green pepper, seeded and
  quartered
2 hard-cooked eggs, peeled

1 can (7-ounce) tuna fish
4 sweet pickles
4 tablespoons mayonnaise
8 slices white or rye bread or toast

1. Place Blade in Bowl; process to chop scallions, celery and green pepper finely. Add eggs, tuna fish, pickles and mayonnaise. Pulse on and off to blend.
2. Spread generously on bread or toast.

Makes 4 sandwiches.

Shrimp Salad Sandwiches

Keep these sandwiches well chilled.

2 ribs celery, cut in 1-inch pieces
2 cans (6½ ounce each) shrimp,
  well drained

4 tablespoons mayonnaise
1 tablespoon mustard
Buttered white bread or soft rolls

1. Place Blade in Bowl; process celery until finely chopped. Add shrimp, mayonnaise and mustard. Pulse on and off until mixture is blended.
2. Spread on bread or rolls.

Makes 4 sandwiches.

VARIATIONS:

Lobster or crabmeat may be substituted for the shrimp.

French Chef Salad Sandwiches

2 medium tomatoes, halved
2 hard-cooked eggs, halved
1 medium head iceberg lettuce, quartered
4 ounces sharp Cheddar cheese, cut to fit Feed Tube
4 ounces Swiss cheese, cut to fit Feed Tube
8 ounces salami, cut to fit Feed Tube
6 small French bread loaves

1. Place Blade in Bowl. Process to coarsely chop tomatoes; remove to a mixing bowl.
2. Process to coarsely chop eggs; add to tomatoes.
3. Place Disc, slice side up, in Bowl. Slice lettuce; add to mixing bowl ingredients. Slice cheeses and salami; set aside.
4. For each sandwich, cut top from bread loaf; remove center from bottom half of bread. Fill with salad mixture. Top with meat and cheese slices and top half of bread.

Makes 6 sandwiches.

NOTE

Bread removed from center of loaf can be processed to make crumbs.

Breads & Rolls

Lucky people come home to the aroma of baking, and even luckier are those who do the baking.

This section has recipes for yeast breads, pizza and rolls, which rise mainly with the help of yeast, and quick breads, muffins, scones and popovers, which rise with baking powder, baking soda or eggs.

Your food processor will do the kneading much faster than you can do it by hand, and generally speed your progress. But, read Tips for Better Bread Baking (see Index) before you begin.

Sour Cream Herb Bread

An aromatic yet slightly tart bread that tastes even better the day after baking!

2 cups flour
1 teaspoon baking powder
½ teaspoon baking soda
½ teaspoon salt
1 teaspoon dill
½ teaspoon each oregano, thyme, basil and tarragon

1 tablespoon each parsley and chives (optional)
1 cup sour cream
2 eggs
⅓ cup honey
4 tablespoons melted butter or margarine

1. Process flour, baking powder, baking soda, salt and herbs for 10 seconds. Add sour cream. Process for 10 seconds. Scrape sides down.
2. With processor running, pour eggs, honey and butter through Feed Tube.
3. Pour into greased 9 x 5-inch pan. Bake in preheated 350° F. oven for 45 minutes. Cool on wire rack.

Makes 1 loaf.

Golden Pumpkin Bread

A light-colored and delicately textured bread.

½ cup blanched almonds
1¾ cup flour
1 cup sugar
½ teaspoon baking powder
1 teaspoon baking soda
1 teaspoon salt
1 teaspoon grated orange rind

½ teaspoon each nutmeg and ginger
½ cup butter or margarine, cut into 4 pieces
2 eggs
1 cup canned pumpkin
¼ cup milk

1. Place Blade in Bowl; chop nuts and set aside.
2. Process flour, sugar, baking powder, baking soda, salt, rind and spices for 10 seconds. Add pumpkin and butter pieces and process for 10 seconds.
3. With processor running, pour eggs and milk through Feed Tube. Scrape sides down.
4. Add nuts; process just enough to mix.
5. Pour into a greased 9 x 5-inch pan. Bake in preheated 350° F. oven 60 to 70 minutes. Cool on wire rack.

Makes 1 loaf.

VARIATIONS:

Pumpkin Raisin Muffins—Omit nuts and substitute ½ cup of raisins. Decrease milk to ¾ of a cup, butter to ¼ of a cup and use only 1 egg. Spoon batter into greased muffin pan. Bake in a preheated 375° F. oven 30 minutes. Serve hot.

Makes 12 muffins.

Green Chili & Cheese Cornbread

A spicy bread to serve with a chicken or fish dinner.

4 ounces Monterey Jack cheese
½ cup flour
2 teaspoons baking powder
1 teaspoon baking soda
¼ teaspoon paprika
1½ cups cornmeal

⅓ cup packed brown sugar
1 egg
1 cup sour cream
**1 (4-ounce) can drained green
   chilies**

1. Place Disc, shred side up, in Bowl; shred cheese and set aside.
2. Place Blade in Bowl; process flour, baking powder, baking soda, paprika, cornmeal and brown sugar for 10 seconds. Add sour cream and egg. Process for 10 seconds. Scrape sides down.
3. Add chilies and cheese; process just until blended.
4. Pour into greased 8-inch square pan. Bake in preheated 350° F. oven 30 minutes. Serve warm with butter or cool on rack.

Makes 1 loaf.

Carrot Fruit Spice Bread

*Full of so many flavors and exceptionally moist. Next time, substitute
½-pound zucchini for the carrots.*

½ pound fresh carrots
1½ cups flour
1 cup sugar
1 teaspoon baking soda
½ teaspoon salt
½ teaspoon baking powder
1 teaspoon cinnamon
¼ teaspoon nutmeg

**½ cup butter or margarine, cut
   into 8 pieces**
2 eggs
1 teaspoon vanilla extract
½ cup currants
½ cup pecans
**½ cup well-drained, crushed
   pineapple**

1. Place Disc, shred side up, in Bowl; shred carrots and set aside.
2. Place Blade in Bowl; process flour, sugar, baking soda, salt, baking powder, spices and butter for 15 seconds.
3. With processor running, pour eggs and vanilla through Feed Tube. Scrape sides down.
4. Add carrots, currants, pecans and pineapple. Process just enough to thoroughly blend ingredients.
5. Pour into a greased 9 x 5-inch pan. Bake in preheated 350° F. oven 65 minutes, until toothpick or knife inserted in center comes out clean. Cool in pan 10 minutes, then remove and cool on wire rack.

Makes 1 loaf.

"Love 'Em" Bran Muffins

We tried many recipes and these are the best bran muffins you'll ever taste...a delicious way to incorporate fiber into your diet.

1 cup flour
1 cup unprocessed bran
1 teaspoon baking soda
½ teaspoon grated orange rind
   (optional)
¼ cup brown sugar

½ cup butter or margarine, cut into
   4 pieces
1 cup sour cream
¼ cup molasses
1 egg
½ cup raisins

1. Place Blade in Bowl; process flour, bran, baking soda, orange rind and sugar for 5 seconds. Add butter and sour cream; process for 10 seconds.
2. With processor running, pour molasses and egg through Feed Tube. Scrape sides down.
3. Add raisins and pulse on and off to mix.
4. Spoon batter into greased muffin pan. Bake in preheated 400° F. oven 20 minutes. Serve hot with butter.

Makes 12 muffins.

Anadama Muffins

An old American favorite...try some marmalade on a hot muffin.

1 cup cornmeal
1½ cups flour
½ teaspoon baking soda
2 teaspoons baking powder
¼ teaspoon salt
Dash of cinnamon

1½ cups sour cream
1 egg
4 tablespoons melted butter or
   margarine
¼ cup molasses

1. Place Blade in Bowl; process cornmeal, flour, baking soda, baking powder, salt and cinnamon for about 5 seconds. Add sour cream; process for 10 seconds.
2. With processor running, pour egg, butter and molasses through Feed Tube. Process just enough to mix.
3. Spoon batter into greased muffin pan.
4. Bake in a preheated 400° F. oven 25 minutes.

Makes 12 muffins.

Day Chippers

Two favorite flavors get kids to eat something in the morning. Pack one for lunch too.

2 cups flour
½ cup sugar
1½ teaspoons baking powder
½ teaspoon baking soda
½ teaspoon salt
1 tablespoon grated orange rind

½ cup butter, cut into 8 pieces
¾ cup peanut butter
1 egg
1 cup milk
1 cup chocolate chips

1. Place Blade in Bowl; process flour, sugar, baking powder, baking soda, salt, orange rind, butter and peanut butter till blended, about 15 seconds.
2. With processor running, pour egg and milk through Feed Tube. Scrape sides down.
3. Add chocolate chips; process just enough to mix.
4. Spoon into greased muffin pan. Bake in a preheated 375° F. oven 25 minutes. Cool on wire rack.

Makes 12 muffins

VARIATION:
To make bread, pour batter into greased loaf and bake in preheated 350° F. oven 65 minutes.

Cheddar-Onion Scones

Buttermilk gives this variation on traditional American biscuits a tangy flavor.

4 ounces Cheddar cheese
1 small onion, quartered
2½ cups flour
½ teaspoon baking soda
2 teaspoons baking powder

¼ teaspoon salt
¼ cup butter, cut into 4 pieces
⅔ cup buttermilk
2 tablespoons cream

1. Place Disc, shred side up, in Bowl; shred cheese and set aside.
2. Place Blade in Bowl; process to finely chop onion. Add flour, baking soda, baking powder and salt. Process about 10 seconds. Add butter pieces. Process until mixture resembles coarse crumbs, about 10 seconds.
3. With processor running, pour buttermilk and cream through Feed Tube.
4. Sprinkle grated cheese over dough. Process just enough to blend. Dough will be sticky.
5. Turn onto lightly floured surface. Roll out to 6 x 8-inch rectangle, using extra flour if necessary. Cut into 2 x 2-inch squares. Place on greased baking sheet. Bake in a preheated 375° F. oven 20 minutes. Serve warm with butter or margarine.

Makes 12 scones.

VARIATION:
Raisin Scones—Omit onion and cheese. Add 5 tablespoons of sugar. Increase butter to ½ cup. Decrease buttermilk to ⅓ cup and mix in 2 eggs. Blend in ½ cup raisins. Continue as above.

Popovers

Rarities in most kitchens yet so simple to prepare. The hot-oven method imparts a crusty outside and moist yet firm inside.

3 eggs
1 cup milk
½ teaspoon salt

1 tablespoon melted butter or
   margarine
1 cup flour

1. Place Blade in Bowl; process eggs, milk, salt, butter for 5 seconds. Sprinkle flour in bowl. Process 10 seconds. Scrape sides down. Process 5 seconds.
2. Ladle batter into greased muffin pan or 6-cup popover pan.
3. Bake in a preheated 425° F. oven 30 minutes until brown and crispy. To test for doneness, sides should be firm. Insert knife on side to let steam escape. Serve immediately with butter.

Makes 6 large or 12 small popovers.

VARIATION:

Cheese Popovers: add 2 ounces shredded cheese.

YEAST
BREADS

French Bread

True French Bread has only the basics. Try ours with Potted Shrimp (see Index) or, at your next barbecue, try Bruscetta (below).

1 package yeast
1 cup warm water, divided
1½ teaspoons salt
2¾ cups flour

1. Place Blade in Bowl. Dissolve yeast and ¼ cup of the warm water in bowl. Allow to stand for about 3 minutes. Add the salt and all the flour. Process for 5 to 10 seconds.
2. With processor running; pour remaining water through Feed Tube. Process till dough forms a ball and turns in bowl 25 times. Turn dough onto lightly floured surface.
3. Knead about 10 times. Place in floured bowl, cover with towel and let rise in warm place for 1½ to 2 hours.
4. Punch down. Shape into a 14-inch long strand. Place in greased baquette pan or on greased baking sheet. Let rise for about 1 hour.
5. Diagonally score the top 3 times with steel blade or knife. Bake in a preheated 425° F. oven for 30 minutes. Place ice cubes in a pan on the oven floor (the steam produces a thin, crisp crust). Reduce heat to 400° F. and bake an additional 10 minutes. Cool on wire rack.

Makes 1 loaf.

SUGGESTION:

Bruscetta—cut bread into thick slices. Cut 2 or 3 garlic cloves in half. Rub each side with garlic. Sprinkle both sides with wine vinegar, olive oil and salt. Toast on an open grill. Serve while waiting for the rest of the meal.

Make-It-Yourself Pizza

No time to cook? Keep these handy. They can be used for a quick hot dinner or snack.

1 package yeast	**1 teaspoon salt**
¾ cup + 2 tablespoons warm	**1 tablespoon oil**
water, divided	**2¾ cup flour**
2 teaspoons sugar	

1. In a measuring cup dissolve yeast in ¼ cup water. Add sugar and let stand for 3 minutes.
2. Place Blade in Bowl; add all the flour and salt in Bowl; process for 10 seconds. With processor running pour yeast mixture through Feed Tube.
3. Gradually pour in remaining water and oil. Process till dough forms a ball and turns in bowl about 25 times. Let dough stand 2 minutes. Process 15 seconds.
4. Turn into lightly floured bowl; cover with towel and let rise in warm place for 45 minutes.
5. Punch down. Divide into 4 pieces. Roll and shape each into a 7-inch round. Place on ungreased baking sheet. Bake in preheated 350° F. oven 10 minutes. Cool, then wrap and store in refrigerator. To serve, place on ungreased pan, top with your favorite fillings.*
6. Bake in a preheated 425° F. oven 20 to 25 minutes.

Makes 4 (7-inch) pizza rounds.

* *Keep covered containers of sliced peppers, chopped onions, tomato sauce, sliced pepperoni and salami, and several kinds of shredded cheeses in your refrigerator. Be daring and make up your own toppings!*

Onion 'Burger Buns

Ordinary hamburgers taste extraordinary encased in homemade buns with subtle onion flavor! If you wish sprinkle the tops with sesame seeds.

1 medium onion, quartered
½ cup warm water, divided
1 package yeast
1 tablespoon sugar
2¾ cups flour
2 tablespoons instant nonfat dry milk

1 teaspoon salt
3 tablespoons butter or margarine, cut in half
1 egg beaten

1. In a measuring cup, dissolve ¼ cup warm water and yeast. Add sugar and let stand 3 minutes.
2. Place Blade in Bowl; finely chop onion. Remove and set aside 3 tablespoons for bun tops. Add the flour, dry milk, salt and 1½ tablespoons butter or margarine to the chopped onion. Process till blended, about 15 seconds. With processor running pour in the yeast mixture. Process in 10 seconds.
3. Add 2 tablespoons of the beaten egg to the onion and set aside. With processor running pour remaining egg and water through Feed Tube. Process till dough forms a ball and turns in bowl 25 times. Let dough stand for 2 minutes. Process 15 seconds more.
4. Place dough in lightly floured bowl, cover with towel and let rise in warm place for 45 minutes. Punch down.
5. Divide into 8 to 10 pieces. Shape each into a smooth ball and place on greased baking sheet. Flatten balls. Let rise in warm place for 30 minutes.
6. Melt remaining 1½ tablespoons butter or margarine. Combine with egg-onion mixture. Brush on buns. Bake in a preheated 375° F. oven 20 to 25 minutes. Cool on wire rack.

Makes 8 to 10 buns.

Pita's Wheat Pockets

Pack these loaves with one of our sandwich fillings or salads.

1 cup warm water, divided	2 cups all-purpose flour
1 package yeast	1 cup whole wheat flour
½ tablespoon sugar	1 teaspoon salt

1. In a measuring cup, dissolve yeast in ¼ of the water. Sprinkle in sugar and let stand for 3 minutes.
2. Place Blade in Bowl. Add all the flours and salt and process until blended, about 10 seconds.
3. With processor running slowly pour yeast mixture through Feed Tube. Slowly pour in remaining ¾ cup of water. Process until dough forms a ball that cleans the sides of the bowl and turns around 25 times. Let dough stand 2 minutes. Process 15 seconds.
4. Place dough on lightly floured counter, cover and let rest 30 minutes. Punch down. Divide into 3 pieces. Roll each into an 8-inch round; place on lightly floured baking sheet.
5. Bake on lowest rack of a preheated 475° F. oven 5 to 7 minutes. Place under broiler for 1 minute to brown tops. Remove and cool on rack. To use, cut each in half and fill.

Makes 6 half-loaves.

Raisin Oat Bread

A wholesome bread suitable for sandwiches and toasting. And no one will miss the salt.

¾ cup warm water, divided	1 tablespoon butter or margarine
1 package yeast	1 teaspoon cinnamon
2 tablespoons molasses	½ cup raisins
2 cups flour	½ cup melted butter or margarine
¾ cup old-fashioned or quick-cooking oats	

1. In a measuring cup, dissolve yeast in ¼ cup of the water. Add molasses and let stand for 3 minutes.
2. Place Blade in Bowl; add flour, oats, butter and cinnamon. Process about 15 seconds. With processor running, pour in yeast mixture through Feed Tube. Process about 10 seconds.
3. With processor running, pour remaining water through Feed Tube. Process until dough forms a ball and turns in bowl 25 times. Let dough stand for 2 minutes. Process again; dough should turn in bowl 15 times.
4. Knead in raisins. Place in lightly floured bowl, cover and let rise in warm place, about 1 hour.
5. Punch down. Place in greased 8½ x 4½-inch loaf pan or round 1 quart soufflé dish. Let rise 1 hour in warm place.
6. Brush with melted butter. Bake in a preheated 375° F. oven 35 minutes.

Makes 1 loaf.

VARIATION:

Raisin Bran Bread—Increase flour to 2¼ cups. Substitute ¾ cup of raw, unprocessed bran for the oats.

Tomato Gruyere Bread

A surprisingly delicious blending of flavors. The color is especially pretty too. Serve toasted with your favorite soup.

¼ cup warm water	1-2 cloves garlic
1 package yeast	2 tablespoons butter or margarine
1 tablespoon sugar	⅓ cup V-8 or tomato juice
2¾ cups flour	1 egg
½ teaspoon salt	6 ounces Gruyere cheese

1. Place Disc, shred side up, in Bowl. Shred cheese; remove and set aside. In a measuring cup dissolve yeast in warm water. Sprinkle in sugar and allow to stand for 3 minutes.
2. Place Blade in Bowl; process flour, salt and garlic and butter until blended. With processor running, pour yeast mixture through Feed Tube.
3. With processor running, pour juice and egg through Feed Tube. Process until dough forms a ball that turns around in bowl 25 times. Turn out onto lightly floured surface. Knead in all but 2 tablespoons of the cheese.
4. Place in floured bowl, cover, and let rise 1 hour in warm place. Punch down. Shape and place in greased 9 x 5-inch pan or in greased 1-quart soufflé dish. Let rise 30 minutes.
5. Sprinkle top with remaining cheese. Bake in a preheated 350° F. oven 35 minutes. Cool on wire rack.

Makes 1 loaf.

Rosemary Wheat Bread

Vary the herbs each time you make this fine-textured bread.

¼ cup warm water	1 tablespoon rosemary
1 package yeast	1½ cups all-purpose flour
3 tablespoons sugar	¾ cup whole wheat flour
¼ cup butter or margarine, cut into 4 pieces	1 egg
1 teaspoon salt	5 tablespoons milk

1. In a measuring cup, dissolve yeast in warm water. Sprinkle in 1 tablespoon of the sugar.
2. Place Blade in Bowl; process remaining sugar, butter, salt, rosemary and flours until blended, about 15 seconds. With processor running pour yeast mixture through Feed Tube.
3. With processor running, pour egg and milk through Feed Tube. Process until dough forms a ball that turns around in the bowl 25 times. Let dough stand 2 minutes. Process until dough turns 15 more times.
4. Turn into lightly floured bowl, cover and let rise in warm place 1 hour. Punch down. Place in greased 8½ x 4½-inch pan. Let rise 45 minutes.
5. Brush top with melted butter, if desired. Bake in a preheated 375° F. oven 35 minutes. Cool on rack.

Makes 1 loaf.

Challah

A traditional bread for everyday eating. It makes a rich and flavorful French Toast.

¾ cup warm water, divided	1 teaspoon salt
1 package yeast	1 egg
1 tablespoon sugar	1 egg yolk
2¾ cups flour	2 tablespoons water
1 tablespoon butter or margarine	Poppy or sesame seeds

1. In a measuring cup, dissolve yeast in ¼ cup warm water. Sprinkle sugar in and let stand 3 minutes.
2. Place Blade in Bowl; process flour, butter, and salt until blended. With processor running, pour yeast mixture through Feed Tube.
3. With processor running slowly pour in egg and remaining warm water through Feed Tube. Process until dough forms a ball that turns in bowl 25 times. Let dough stand 2 minutes. Process until dough turns around 15 times.
4. Turn into lightly floured bowl, cover and let rise in warm place for 1 hour. Punch down.
5. Divide into 3 equal parts. Shape each into an 18-inch strand. Braid loosely together. Tuck ends under and place on greased baking sheet (or, for a higher loaf, place in greased 9 x 5-inch pan). Let rise 45 minutes.
6. Combine egg yolk and water. Brush over braid. Sprinkle with seeds. Bake in a preheated 375° F. oven 30 minutes. Remove and cool on rack.

Makes 1 loaf

Crisp Dinner Rolls

For a softer crumb, dissolve yeast as directed but substitute milk for the remaining water. Also, create your own shapes.

¾ to 1 cup warm water, divided	1 teaspoon salt
1 package yeast	Melted butter or margarine
1 tablespoon sugar	(optional)
2¾ cups flour	Poppy or Sesame seeds (optional)
2 tablespoons butter or margarine	

1. In a measuring cup dissolve yeast in ¼ cup or the warm water. Sprinkle in sugar and let stand 3 minutes.
2. Place Blade in Bowl; process flour, butter and salt until blended. With processor running pour yeast mixture through Feed Tube. Slowly pour in remaining water. Process until dough forms a ball that turns in bowl 25 times. Let stand 2 minutes. Process until dough turns around 15 times.
3. Turn into lightly floured bowl, cover and let rise in warm place 1 hour. Punch down.
4. Divide dough into 12 pieces and form into your favorite rolls (cloverleafs, knots, etc.). Let rise in warm place for 30 minutes. Bake in a preheated 400° F. oven 15 minutes. Serve hot with butter.

Makes 12 rolls.

Orange Rye Bread

A very different rye bread, much lighter and sweeter than others. The egg white and water will give you a chewy top crust.

¼ cup + ⅔ cup warm water, divided
1 package yeast
3 tablespoons brown sugar
1 tablespoon molasses
1 tablespoon butter or margarine
1 teaspoon salt
1 tablespoon grated orange rind
⅔ cup rye flour
2 cups all-purpose flour
1 egg white, beaten
1 tablespoon cold water

1. In a measuring cup dissolve yeast in ¼ cup warm water. Sprinkle in 1 tablespoon brown sugar and let stand aside 3 minutes.
2. Place Blade in Bowl; process remaining sugar, molasses, butter, salt, orange rind and flours until blended, about 15 seconds. With processor running, pour yeast mixture through Feed Tube. Slowly pour in remaining warm water. Process until dough forms a ball that turns around in bowl 25 times. Let stand 2 minutes. Process again letting dough turn 15 times.
3. Turn into lightly floured bowl, cover and let rise in warm place for 1 hour; punch down.
4. Shape into smooth ball and place on greased baking sheet or in greased loaf pan. Let rise 45 minutes. Brush with beaten egg white and water. Bake in a preheated 375° F. oven 35 minutes. Cool on rack.

Makes 1 loaf.

VARIATION:

Rye Caraway Pull Aparts—Coat bottom of 9-inch square pan with melted butter. Sprinkle with caraway seeds. Shape dough into 12 balls. Let rise 30 minutes. Brush tops with melted butter and sprinkle with caraway seeds. Bake in preheated 375° F. oven 25 minutes.

Basic Sweet Roll Dough

An American favorite! Shape this into coffeecakes or rolls, adding nuts, chocolate chips, raisins or candied fruits.

¼ cup + 3 tablespoons warm
  water, divided
¼ cup sugar
1 package yeast
½ cup instant nonfat dry milk

¼ cup butter or margarine, cut
  into 4 pieces
1 teaspoon salt
2¾ cups flour
2 eggs

1. In a measuring cup dissolve yeast in ¼ cup warm water. Sprinkle in 1 tablespoon sugar and let stand 3 minutes.
2. Place Blade in Bowl; process remaining sugar, milk, butter or margarine, salt and flour until blended, about 15 seconds. With processor running, pour in yeast mixture.
3. Slowly pour eggs and remaining warm water through Feed Tube. Process until dough forms a ball that turns around in bowl 25 times. Let stand 2 minutes. Process again, allowing dough to turn 15 times.
4. Turn dough into lightly floured bowl, cover and let rise in warm place 1 hour; punch down.
5. Proceed to make Cinnamon Raisin Rolls or Date Tea Ring (see following recipes).

Cinnamon Raisin Rolls

1 recipe Basic Sweet Roll Dough
  (see previous recipe)
¼ cup butter or margarine,
  softened

½ cup sugar
1 tablespoon cinnamon
⅓ cup raisins
Melted butter or margarine

1. Roll dough into 18 x 9-inch rectangle. Spread butter or margarine over dough. Combine sugar, cinnamon and raisins. Sprinkle over butter.
2. Starting on long side, roll up. Seal sides firmly. Cut into 12 equal rolls. Arrange, cut side down, in greased 13 x 9-inch pan.
3. Let rise 1 hour.
4. Brush with butter. Bake in a preheated 375° F. oven 20 minutes. Invert on rack and cool to lukewarm before serving. If desired, frost with Confectioners' Sugar Icing (see Index).

Makes 12 rolls.

Date Tea Ring

1 recipe Basic Sweet Roll Dough
  (see Index)
1 (8-ounce) package chopped,
  pitted dates
2 tablespoons brown sugar

⅓ cup water
½ cup walnuts
½ cup butter or margarine,
  softened

1. While dough is rising combine dates, sugar and water in small saucepan. Cook over medium heat, stirring constantly, until water is absorbed, about 2 minutes. Remove from heat. Stir in nuts.
2. Cool. Roll dough into a 9 x 15-inch rectangle. Spread with butter. Spread dates over butter. Starting on long side, roll up. Arrange in a circle, seam side down, on greased baking sheet. Pinch ends together to seal. Cut ⅔ of the way through at 1-inch intervals, turning slices on sides. Let rise in warm place for 1 hour.
3. Bake in a preheated 350° F. oven 25 minutes. Cool on wire rack. If desired, frost with Confectioners' Icing (see Index).

Makes 6 to 8 servings.

Coffee Braid

An impressive sweet bread.

¼ cup warm water
1 package yeast
¼ cup sugar
2⅓ cups flour
¼ cup butter or margarine, cut
  into 4 pieces

1 egg
½ teaspoon salt
5 tablespoons milk
Poppy Seed or Lemon Cheese or
  Apricot Filling (see following
  recipes)
Confectioners' sugar

1. In a measuring cup dissolve yeast in water. Sprinkle in 1 tablespoon sugar and let stand 3 minutes.
2. Place Blade in Bowl; add flour, remaining sugar, butter and salt. Process until mixed. With processor running, pour yeast mixture through Feed Tube.
3. Add egg and milk. Continue processing until dough forms a ball and turns in bowl 25 times. Let stand 2 minutes. Process until ball turns around 15 times. Turn into lightly floured bowl, cover and let rise in warm place 30 minutes.
4. Punch down. Roll out into a 10 x 15-inch rectangle. Place on greased baking sheet.
5. Spread with desired Filling lengthwise down center of ⅓ of dough. Cut sides of dough at 1-inch intervals to within ½ inch of filling. Fold strips over filling, alternating from side to side.
6. Let rise in warm place for 30 minutes. Bake in a preheated 350° F. oven 30 minutes. Cool on wire rack. Sprinkle with Confectioners' sugar.

Makes 1 coffee braid.

POPPY SEED FILLING

¾ cup poppy seeds
¾ cup whole almonds
1 tablespoon grated lemon peel
½ cup sugar

⅓ cup milk
3 tablespoons butter or margarine
1 tablespoons lemon juice

1. Place Blade in Bowl; process poppy seeds, almonds and lemon rind until mixture is the consistency of cornmeal, about 2 minutes.
2. Pour in saucepan. Add sugar, milk, butter and lemon juice. Cook over low heat, stirring frequently, until thickened, about 10 minutes. Cool.

LEMON CHEESE FILLING

11 ounces cream cheese, softened and cut into chunks
½ cup sugar

1 egg
1 teaspoon grated lemon rind
½ cup golden raisins

1. Place Blade in Bowl; process cream cheese, sugar, egg and lemon rind until smooth. Add raisins. Pulse on and off to mix. Proceed as above.
2. Bake in a preheated 375° F. oven 25 minutes.

APRICOT FILLING

1¼ cups dried apricots
¾ cup water
¾ cup packed brown sugar

1. Place Blade in Bowl; chop apricots.
2. Place in saucepan along with water and brown sugar. Bring to a boil, then cook until liquid is absorbed, about 20 minutes. Proceed as above.
3. Bake in a preheated 375° F. oven 25 minutes.

Poteca

An old European treasure (pronounced "Po-teet-sa") suitable for special occasions.

¼ cup warm water
1 package yeast
¼ cup sugar
3 cups flour
½ teaspoon salt
¼ cup butter or margarine, cut into
  4 pieces

¼ cup milk
2 eggs
Walnut Filling (below)
Melted butter or margarine
Confectioners' sugar

1. In a measuring cup, dissolve yeast in warm water. Sprinkle in 1 tablespoon of the sugar and allow to stand for 3 minutes.
2. Place Blade in Bowl; add all the flour, remaining sugar, salt and butter; process for 10 seconds. With processor running, pour yeast mixture through Feed Tube; process 10 seconds.
3. With the processor running, pour milk and eggs through the Feed Tube. Dough should form a ball that cleans the sides of the bowl. Process until ball turns around 25 times. Let stand 2 minutes. Process until dough turns around in bowl 15 times.
4. Place dough in lightly floured bowl, cover with towel and let rise in warm place for 1½ hours. Prepare Walnut Filling while dough rises.
5. Punch down; roll out dough on well-floured surface, using more flour, if necessary, to keep dough from sticking. Roll out to a 20 x 15-inch rectangle. Spread with filling. Starting at long side, roll up jelly roll fashion; seal edges. Gently stretch dough to a 23-inch roll. Place in a "U" shape, seam side down, on greased baking sheet. Let rise in warm place for 1 hour.
6. Bake in a preheated 325° F. oven 35 minutes, Place on a wire rack. Brush with melted butter and sprinkle with Confectioners' sugar.

Makes 1 loaf.

WALNUT FILLING

6 tablespoons cream or milk
½ cup packed brown sugar
¼ cup butter or margarine, cut
  in 4 pieces
1 tablespoon honey

1 teaspoon vanilla or orange
  extract
2 teaspoons grated orange rind
2 cups walnuts

Place Blade in Bowl. Put all ingredients except nuts in bowl and process until blended. Add in nuts and continue processing until finely chopped.

Pecan Sticky Buns

Melt-in-your-mouth rich buns—a delicious way to say "Good Morning."

½ cup warm water, divided
1 package yeast
¼ cup sugar
2¼ cups flour
2 tablespoons instant nonfat dry
  milk

1 teaspoon salt
1 egg
Pecan Topping, below
2 tablespoons melted butter
  or margarine

1. In measuring cup dissolve yeast in ¼ cup water. Sprinkle in 1 tablespoon of the sugar and let stand 3 minutes.
2. Place Blade in Bowl; add flour, remaining sugar, milk solids and salt. Process 10 seconds. With processor running, pour yeast mixture through Feed Tube.
3. With processor running, pour egg and remaining water through Feed Tube. Process until dough forms a ball that cleans the sides of the bowl and turns around 25 times. Let dough stand for 2 minutes. Process until dough turns around in bowl 15 times.
4. Place dough in lightly floured bowl, cover with towel and let rise 30 minutes. Prepare Pecan Topping (below) while dough rises.
5. Pour topping into greased 9-inch cake pan. Punch dough down. Shape into 10 balls, dip in melted butter or margarine and arrange over Topping. Let rise in warm place for 1 hour.
6. Bake in a preheated 375° F. oven 20 minutes. Cool 1 minute in pan, then invert buns onto plate. Serve immediately.

Makes 10 buns.

PECAN TOPPING

¼ cup packed brown sugar
¼ cup butter or margarine
2 tablespoons corn syrup
⅓ cup pecans

1. Place Blade in Bowl; process to coarsely chop nuts.
2. Combine sugar, butter and corn syrup in small saucepan. Cook until bubbly and sugar dissolves.
3. Remove from heat. Stir in nuts.

St. Lucia's Crown

Prepare this attractive Swedish masterpiece at Christmas. If you wish sprinkle with chopped candied fruits.

¼ cup warm water	3 eggs
1 package yeast	¼ cup cream
¼ cup sugar	Pinch of saffron
2¾ cups flour	½ cup golden raisins
¼ cup butter or margarine, cut into 4 pieces	¼ cup blanched almonds
	1 tablespoon cold water
1 teaspoon salt	Confectioners' Sugar Icing (below)

1. In a measuring cup dissolve yeast in warm water. Sprinkle in 1 tablespoon of the sugar and let stand 3 minutes.
2. Place Blade in Bowl; add flour, remaining sugar, butter and salt. Process until mixed, about 15 seconds. With processor running pour yeast mixture and 2 eggs through Feed Tube; process until blended.
3. Stir saffron into 2 tablespoons of milk. With processor running drizzle in enough milk so dough forms a ball. Process until ball turns around 25 times. Turn off and let stand 2 minutes. Process 10 seconds.
4. Knead in raisins. Place in lightly floured bowl, cover and let rise 1½ hours in warm place. Punch down. Divide dough into 3 equal parts and shape ino a 25-inch long strand. Braid together and place on greased baking sheet. Shape into a ring about 8-inches in diameter. Pinch ends together. Let rise 45 minutes.
5. Beat remaining egg with cold water. Brush on ring. Bake in preheated 350° F. oven 25 minutes. Cool on wire rack. Drizzle with Confectioners' Sugar Icing (below). Sprinkle with almonds.

Makes 1 (8-inch) ring.

VARIATION:

Saffron Raisin Buns—Shape dough into 12 balls. Place on greased baking sheet. With Blade or knife, cut a shallow "X" on bun tops. Bake in a preheated 375° F. oven 20 minutes.

Makes 12 buns.

Confectioners' Sugar Icing

1 cup Confectioners' sugar
1 teaspoon butter or margarine,
    softened
2 to 3 tablespoons milk

1. Place Blade in Bowl; process combined ingredients, adding in more milk if necessary.
2. Drizzle over coffeecakes and rolls.

Desserts, Cakes & Pies

For many of us, a meal is incomplete without dessert—a pleasurable treat to conclude the meal.

Your food processor simplifies and cuts short the preparation of the entire repetoire. And it makes tart, light sherbets and ices the easiest desserts imaginable.

Highly recommended in this chapter are: Chocolate Almond Torte, Orange Macaroons, Viennese Apple Strudel, Shaker Lemon Pie, Grapefruit Sherbet and Strawberry Ice Cream Cake.

Brazilian Nut Cakes

½ cup flour
¼ teaspoon salt
1½ cups nuts
2 eggs
1 cup packed brown sugar

1 tablespoon dry instant coffee
¼ teaspoon cinnamon
1 teaspoon vanilla extract
½ cup butter or margarine, melted

1. Preheat oven to 350° F.; sift together flour and salt
2. Place Blade in Bowl; process nuts until finely chopped; set aside.
3. Place Beater Accessory in Bowl; add eggs and beat well, then add sugar, coffee, cinnamon and vanilla. Add flour/salt mixture, melted butter and nuts; blend.
4. Spread batter in a greased 8 x 8 x 2-inch pan. Bake 25 to 30 minutes. Cut in 1-inch squares while warm. (For crisp bars, bake in a 10 x 10-inch pan for about 12 to 15 minutes.)

Makes 36 pieces.

Chocolate Orange Almond Torte

A one-layer cake with a brownie-like texture.

4 ounces semisweet chocolate
1¼ cups whole blanched almonds
2 slices dry bread, in pieces
Rind of 1 orange
8 tablespoons unsalted butter or
   margarine

½ cup sugar
1 tablespoon orange marmalade
1 tablespoon orange liqueur
3 eggs
Confectioners' sugar

1. Preheat oven to 375° F. Grease side of an 8-inch round cake pan. Line the bottom of the pan with waxed paper. Butter the paper; set aside.
2. Melt the chocolate in top of a double boiler; allow to cool.
3. Place Blade in Bowl; process almonds until they are finely ground; set aside. Process bread and orange rind until finely crumbed; set aside.
4. Add butter to Bowl with sugar; cream until well blended and light. Add the preserves, liqueur and eggs; process until well mixed. Add chocolate, ground nuts, orange rind and bread crumbs; blend well.
5. Pour mixture into the prepared pan and bake for 25 minutes. (The cake should be slightly moist in the center.)
6. Cool in its pan on a wire rack. Turn out onto rack and remove the paper.
7. Sprinkle with Confectioners' sugar or frost with Chocolate Nut Frosting (see following recipe).

Makes 1 (8-inch) cake.

Chocolate Nut Frosting

1 ounce unsweetened chocolate
1 teaspoon butter or margarine
1 cup Confectioners' sugar

5 teaspoons hot water
1 cup nuts

1. Melt together chocolate and butter in top of a double boiler. Stir in Confectioners' sugar and hot water, a spoon at a time until frosting can be drizzled over cooled cake.
2. Place Blade in Bowl. Process nuts until finely chopped. Combine with frosting.

Makes about 1 cup.

Walnut Cream Cheese Cake

This is a moist cake and will keep several days in the refrigerator, or several months in the freezer.

¼ cup walnuts
1 cup sugar
Rind of ½ lemon, cut in
   small pieces
1 (3-ounce) package cream cheese

½ cup butter or margarine
3 eggs
1 cup flour
1 teaspoon baking powder
1 teaspoon vanilla extract

1. Place Blade in Bowl; add walnuts and process until finely chopped.
2. Replace Blade in Bowl; add ¼ cup of the sugar and lemon rind. Process to finely grind the lemon rind. Add cream cheese, butter and remaining sugar; process until smooth. Add eggs, one at a time, and process until mixture is fluffy.
3. Sift flour and baking powder together and add to the mixture; process to blend. Add vanilla and blend.
4. Pour batter into a greased and floured 9 x 9 x 2-inch baking pan. Bake in a preheated 350° F. oven for 60 minutes, or until top is lightly browned. Remove from oven and cool at room temperature.

Makes 12 servings.

Strawberry Cheesecake

A beauty of a cake.

Graham cracker crust
1 envelope unflavored gelatin
¼ cup cold water
Rind of ½ lemon, cut in
   small pieces
½ cup sugar
1 (8-ounce) package cream cheese

¼ cup flour
¾ cup milk
¼ cup lemon juice
1 cup heavy cream
1 quart fresh strawberries
1 (16-ounce) jar apple jelly

1. Prepare crust and press on the bottom of a springform pan.
2. Soften gelatin in cold water; stir over low heat to dissolve.
3. Replace Blade in Bowl; add lemon rind and ¼ cup of the sugar. Process until rind is finely grated. Add cream cheese, remaining sugar, flour, milk, lemon juice and gelatin; chill until slightly thickened.
4. Place Beater Accessory in Bowl; whip cream until it forms soft peaks. Fold cream into cheese mixture; pour over crust. Refrigerate until firm.
5. Place Blade in Bowl; slice strawberries (reserve a few for decoration). In a saucepan, melt apple jelly. Cool and stir in strawberries. Remove rim of pan; top with fruit.

Makes 8 to 10 servings.

Almond Cookies

Crisp, golden cookies for a party platter.

1 cup blanched almonds
2 cups flour
½ cup sugar
½ cup brown sugar
1 teaspoon cinnamon
½ teaspoon nutmeg
½ teaspoon salt

1 teaspoon almond extract
½ cup vegetable shortening,
   chilled, cut in pieces
½ cup butter or margarine
½ cup milk
3 eggs, separated
36 whole almonds

1. Place Blade in Bowl. Process almonds until finely ground. Add flour, sugar, seasonings, shortening, butter and egg yolks; process until blended. With processor running, pour milk through Feed Tube until a ball forms.
2. Wrap dough and place in refrigerator for 2 hours.
3. Preheat oven to 350° F. Form dough into 1-inch balls. Place on ungreased cookie sheets. Flatten balls with the bottom of a glass. Brush tops of cookies with beaten egg whites. Press 1 almond on top of each cookie. Bake 15 to 20 minutes, or until light brown. Remove to rack to cool.

Makes about 3 dozen.

Macaroons

The perfect cookie with a bowl of fresh strawberries or pineapple.

1 cup Almond Paste (see Index)	1 teaspoon vanilla extract
1 cup sugar	1 teaspoon almond extract
	2 egg whites

1. Place Blade in Bowl; process almond paste until it is crumbly. Add sugar, vanilla and almond extracts; process until well blended. With processor running, pour egg whites through Feed Tube; process until dough ball forms.
2. Drop by teaspoonfuls on greased cookie sheets. Bake in a 325° F. oven 20 to 30 minutes, or until light brown. Cool on racks. Use a spatula to remove cookies.

Makes 30 cookies.

VARIATIONS:

Orange Macaroons—Add a 1 x 3-inch strip of orange rind, cut in pieces, to ½ cup of the sugar; process until rind is finely grated. Reduce vanilla to ½ teaspoon.

Chocolate Coconut Macaroons—Add 1 square unsweetened chocolate, melted and 1 (4-ounce) package sweet cooking chocolate, melted, plus the meat of ½ a small coconut, shredded. Reduce sugar to ½ cup.

Marzipan

In Jerusalem, marzipan is considered "the richest food on earth," and is given to a woman just after she has her baby to make their lives sweet.

1¼ cups blanched almonds, divided	1 tablespoon lemon juice
1½ cups sugar	1 egg white, whisked to soft peaks
1 cup water	Blanched almonds, halved

1. Place Blade in Bowl. Process almonds until they are very finely ground.
2. In a heavy saucepan, cook sugar and water over medium heat. Stir with a wooden spoon. When mixture begins to bubble, add several drops of the lemon juice, to keep it from sugaring. Continue cooking and stirring until the mixture is syrupy. Lower the heat; add the ground almonds, and continue stirring and scraping around the edges until the mixture can be formed into a ball and is the consistency of a soft dough. Quickly stir in the remaining lemon juice. Cool slightly.
3. Fold in egg white. Cool completely, stirring from time to time.
4. Shape into small round balls or flatten the dough out with your fingers and cut it into desired shapes with small cookie cutters. Press an almond half on top of each. Store in a plastic bag or airtight container.

Makes approximately 36 pieces.

Almond Paste

1¼ cups blanched almonds
¼ cup cold water

1. Place Blade in Bowl; process almonds ¼ cup at a time until finely ground. Gradually add water until ball forms on the blade. May be wrapped and refrigerated until ready to use.

Makes 1 cup.

Chinese Chews

There are many different recipes with this name; this one is unusually moist and fruity.

2 cups walnuts
1 container (4-ounce) candied orange peel
1 container (4-ounce) candied lemon peel
2 cups flour

½ teaspoon salt (optional)
4 eggs
1 teaspoon vanilla extract
1 package (16-ounces) dark brown sugar
Confectioners' sugar

1. Place Blade in Bowl; process walnuts until coarsely chopped and empty them into a large mixing bowl. Process orange and lemon peel until finely chopped; combine with walnuts along with flour and salt.
2. Place Beater Accessory in Bowl; beat eggs with vanilla until foamy. Add flour-fruit mixture until thoroughly combined. Pour into a lightly greased 13 x 9 x 2-inch baking pan.
3. Bake in a preheated 350° F. oven for 50 minutes, or until a toothpick inserted near center comes out clean. Cool on wire rack. Sprinkle top with Confectioners' sugar. Cut into 1-inch squares.

Makes approximately 5 dozen cookies.

Mocha Walnut Cookies

A blend of coffee, chocolate and dark brown sugar makes the marvelous mocha flavor.

1 cup walnuts
½ cup dark brown sugar
1¾ cups flour
¼ cup cocoa
1 tablespoon dry instant coffee

¼ teaspoon salt
1 cup butter or margarine
2 teaspoons vanilla extract
Confectioners' sugar

1. Place Blade in Bowl. Process to coarsely chop nuts. Add remaining ingredients except Confectioners' sugar; process to blend well.
2. Chill dough for an hour. Shape into 1-inch balls. Place on ungreased cookie sheets. Bake in a preheated 350° F. oven 20 minutes. Remove to rack to cool. While still warm, dust cookies with Confectioners' sugar.

Makes about 2 to 3 dozen.

Apple Ambrosia Pie

Serve warm or at room temperature with ice cream.

¼ cup flour
¼ cup brown sugar, packed
¼ cup walnuts
½ teaspoon cinnamon
⅛ teaspoon salt
3 tablespoons butter or margarine
6 medium-size apples,
   peeled and cored

1 (9-inch) unbaked pie
   shell (see Index)
2 eggs
½ cup sugar
2 tablespoons flour
1 tablespoon lemon juice
¼ teaspoon salt
1 cup sour cream

1. Place Blade in Bowl. Combine ¼ cup flour, brown sugar, walnuts, cinnamon, salt and butter. Process until mixture resembles coarse crumbs. Set aside to use as topping.
2. Place Disc, slice side up, in Bowl; pack apple pieces into Feed Tube. Slice apples. Arrange slices in pastry shell.
3. Return Blade to Bowl. Combine eggs, sugar, 2 tablespoons flour, lemon juice, salt and sour cream. Pulse on and off a few times just to mix. Pour mixture over the apples. Sprinkle with topping.
4. Bake in a 375° F. oven for 35 minutes.

Makes 1 (9-inch) pie.

Chocolate Coconut Pie

Meat of ½ medium fresh coconut,
   peeled and cut into 1-inch pieces
4 ounces German-style sweet
   chocolate
¼ cup butter or margarine
1 can (13-ounce) evaporated milk

3 eggs, slightly beaten
½ cup sugar
Graham Cracker Crust (see Index)
½ cup heavy cream
1 ounce sweet chocolate

1. Place Blade in Bowl; mince coconut, 4 pieces at a time.
2. In a medium saucepan, melt chocolate and butter; add milk, coconut, eggs and sugar and stir until blended; pour into pie crust and bake in a preheated 400° F. oven for 30 minutes.
3. Place Beater Accessory in Bowl; whip cream; spread over top of pie and garnish with grated sweet chocolate.

Makes 1 (9-inch) pie.

Shaker Lemon Pie

Simple, tart and thin.

1 (9-inch) double crust pie shell
   (see Index)
Rind from 2 lemons
1½ cups sugar

3 eggs
2 large lemons, peeled, halved
   and seeded

1. Prepare pastry. Chill. Roll out bottom crust and line a 9-inch pie pan. Keep remaining dough chilled.
2. Place Blade in Bowl; add ¼ cup of the sugar and lemon rind. Process to finely grate rind. Add eggs, remaining sugar and lemon; process to ▪ blend.
3. Pour mixture into unbaked pie shell. Cover with top pastry, sealing edges tightly.
4. Bake 15 minutes in a preheated 425° F. oven; reduce heat to 375° F. for 30 more minutes or until crust is lightly browned.

Makes 1 (9-inch) pie.

Fresh Peach Pie

A mouth-watering pie for your favorite people.

1 (8-inch) double crust pie shell
   (see Index)
3 pounds fresh peaches, peeled,
   pitted and halved
2 teaspoons lemon juice
¾ cup packed brown sugar

½ teaspoon cinnamon
3 tablespoons all-purpose flour
3 tablespoons butter or margarine,
   melted
½ teaspoon nutmeg
¼ teaspoon almond extract

1. Prepare pastry. Chill. Roll out bottom crust and line an 8-inch pie pan. Keep remaining dough chilled. Preheat oven to 400° F.
2. Place Disc, slice side up, in Bowl; slice peaches. Arrange peaches over bottom crust. Sprinkle with lemon juice.
3. Place Blade in Bowl. Process brown sugar, cinnamon, flour, butter, nutmeg and almond extract, pulsing on and off until well mixed and crumbly. Distribute mixture evenly over the peaches.
4. Roll out remaining pastry and cover pie, sealing edges well. Cut several slits in top to vent steam. Bake 15 minutes. Reduce oven temperature to 350° F. and bake 35 to 40 minutes longer until golden. Cover edges with narrow strips of aluminum foil to prevent them from browning too quickly.

Makes 1 (8-inch) pie.

Georgia Pecan Pie

1 cup whole pecans
¼ cup butter or margarine, softened
¾ cup sugar
1 teaspoon vanilla extract
2 tablespoons flour
3 eggs

½ cup coffee-flavored liqueur (optional)
½ cup dark corn syrup
¾ cup evaporated milk
1 (9-inch) pie shell (see Index)
1 cup heavy cream
Pecan halves

1. Place Blade in Bowl; process pecans until finely chopped. Add butter, sugar, vanilla and flour; mix well. With processor running, drop in eggs through the Feed Tube, one at a time. Add the liqueur, corn syrup and evaporated milk.
2. Pour mixture into the pie crust; bake in a preheated 400° F. oven for 10 minutes. Lower oven temperature to 325° F. and bake about 40 minutes, or until firm; chill.
3. When ready to serve, place Beater Accessory in Bowl; whip cream. Garnish pie with whipped cream and pecan halves.

Makes 8 to 9 servings.

New England Pumpkin Nut Pie

A little hard cider, or sherry may be added to the custard for a change of taste.

½ cup pecans
2 cups cooked or canned pumpkin
1 cup brown sugar
⅓ cup heavy cream
4 eggs, separated
½ teaspoon nutmeg

½ teaspoon allspice
½ teaspoon cinnamon
4 tablespoons butter or margarine, melted
1 tablespoon cornstarch
1 unbaked (9-inch) pie

1. Place Blade in Bowl; process to finely chop pecans. Add pumpkin, brown sugar, cream, egg yolks, nutmeg, allspice, cinnamon, and butter. Process until well mixed.
2. Place Beater Accessory in a clean Bowl. Beat egg whites until stiff; add cornstarch and fold into the pumpkin mixture.
3. Pour the filling into the unbaked pie shell, and bake for 10 minutes in a preheated 450° F. oven, then reduce the heat to 350° F. and continue baking for 20 to 25 minutes, or until a knife blade comes out clean. Chill and serve topped with whipped cream if desired.

Makes 1 (9-inch) pie.

Cranberry Tarts

The processor makes this from start to finish.

½ medium orange, unpeeled,
  seeded and cut in small pieces
1 cup sugar
1 egg
2 cups cranberries
4 ounces black walnuts
½ cup raisins

2 tablespoons butter or margarine,
  softened
12 unbaked tart shells (see Index)
½ pint heavy cream
1 teaspoon sugar
½ teaspoon vanilla extract

1. Place Blade in Bowl; add orange pieces, sugar and egg. Process until orange is finely chopped. Add cranberries, raisins and butter and process to finely chop.
2. Spoon mixture into tart shells; bake in a 350° F. oven for 30 to 35 minutes, or until filling is set and crust is brown.
3. Place Beater Accessory in Bowl; whip cream until it peaks. Add sugar and vanilla; spread on tops.

Makes 12 tarts.

Pear and Almond Flan

6 pears, peeled and quartered
½ cup lemon juice
Rind of ½ lemon, cut in small
  pieces
¾ cup sugar
½ cup blanched almonds

1 (10-inch) Sweet Pastry pie
  shell (see Index)
2 eggs
2 tablespoons flour
⅓ cup light cream

1. Place Disc, slice side up, in Bowl; slice pears and empty into a large mixing bowl. Cover with lemon juice and water to prevent darkening.
2. Place Blade in Bowl; add lemon rind, ⅓ cup of the sugar and almonds; process until lemon and almonds are finely chopped.
3. Fill crust with pear slices, starting at the center, and spreading the slices in a spiral pattern. When the bottom of the crust is covered, sprinkle with the sugar mixture. Repeat the procedure ending with a layer of sugar mixture on top.
4. Bake in a 350° F. oven for 20 minutes.
5. Place Blade in Bowl; add eggs, flour, remaining sugar and cream and blend. Drizzle the glaze over the pears; return the pie to the oven and bake 30 minutes longer. Cool to room temperature before serving.

Makes 1 (10-inch) flan.

Viennese Apple Strudel

It helps to play Strauss waltzes while preparing this flaky delicacy.

¼ cup raisins or currants
2 tablespoons dark rum
2 slices dry white bread
2 strips orange rind
2 strips lemon rind
¾ cup blanched almonds
8 medium apples, peeled, cored
¾ cup sugar

1 teaspoon cinnamon
½ teaspoon ground cloves
¼ teaspoon nutmeg
4 tablespoons butter or margarine
6 sheets strudel or fillo dough
1 cup unsalted butter or margarine, melted
Confectioners' sugar

1. Mix raisins with rum. Cover and let stand for at least 2 hours.
2. Place Blade in Bowl; process bread to fine crumbs; set aside. With processor running, drop orange and lemon rind through Feed Tube. Add almonds and process until finely chopped; set aside.
3. Place Disc, slice side up, in Bowl. Pack apples into Feed Tube and slice. Remove apples to a mixing bowl and toss together with ground rind, nuts, sugar, cinnamon, cloves, nutmeg and raisins.
4. In a large skillet, melt 4 tablespoons of butter, add bread crumbs and brown.
5. Place 3 sheets of dough, one on top of the other, on a clean flat surface. Brush each sheet with melted butter and sprinkle ¼ cup of bread crumbs over the entire surface.
6. Place half of the apple mixture, at bottom edge of the dough. Roll dough over the filling, making sure filling stays inside of dough. Fold left edge of the fillo sheet over about 2 inches and brush folded edge with a little butter. Repeat with the right edge of the fillo sheet. Roll the pastry, brushing generously with butter. Place rolled strudel, seam side down, on a lightly greased baking sheet. Brush the top with butter.
7. Repeat the process to make another roll.
8. Bake the rolls in a preheated 375° F. oven for about 45 minutes, or until golden brown. Sprinkle top with Confectioners' sugar. Let strudel cool 1 hour before serving.

Makes 2 rolls (about 24 pieces).

Apple Bread Pudding

An old-time treat, brought into new prominence with the processor to speed things along.

3 slices dry bread, in pieces
8 tablespoons sugar
2 strips lemon peel
2 tablespoons butter or margarine, softened
1 cup milk

½ teaspoon cinnamon
Dash salt
2 eggs separated
3 tart apples, peeled, cored and quartered
½ cup raisins

1. Place Blade in Bowl. Process bread to coarse crumbs; empty into a large mixing bowl. With Blade in Bowl, add 4 tablespoons of the sugar and lemon peel; process to finely grate peel.
2. Add butter, milk, remaining sugar, cinnamon, salt, and egg yolks to Bowl. Pulse on and off to mix; add mixture to the bread crumbs.
3. Chop apples and add along with raisins to other ingredients in mixing bowl.
4. Place Beater Accessory in Bowl; beat egg whites until soft peaks form, then add remaining sugar gradually while continuing to beat until stiff peaks form. Fold egg whites into pudding mixture and turn into an ungreased 1½-quart casserole.
5. Bake in a preheated 350° F. oven 40 to 50 minutes, until a knife inserted into center comes out clean. Cool slightly before serving.

Makes 6 servings.

Chocolate Almond Pots-de-Crème

May be prepared up to 24 hours in advance.

½ cup blanched almonds
1 (6-ounce) package chocolate chips
1 cup light cream, scalded
4 egg yolks

1 tablespoon butter or margarine, softened
2 tablespoons rum
1 cup heavy cream

1. Place Blade in Bowl. Process to finely chop almonds; set aside. Process chocolate chips until finely ground; set aside ¼ cup of grated chocolate to use later. Add light cream, egg yolks, butter and rum. Pulse on and off until mixture is smooth.
2. Pour into pot-de-crème or sherbet glasses, cover with plastic wrap and chill for about 3 hours.
3. Before serving, place Beater Accessory in clean Bowl; whip heavy cream until thick. Gently fold in grated chocolate. Spoon onto tops of chocolate.

Makes 6 servings.

Crumbed Ginger Pears

Chocolate wafers may be substituted in this recipe. They go very well with pears, too.

35 ginger snaps
¼ cup butter or margarine, melted
4 medium pears, cored and halved
Juice of 1 lemon
½ cup packed brown sugar

¼ teaspoon salt
½ teaspoon cinnamon
½ teaspoon nutmeg
¼ cup water
Vanilla ice cream (optional)

1. Place Blade in Bowl; process to crumb cookies. Empty into a mixing bowl and add melted butter. Mix and pat half the crumbs into a 1½-quart baking dish.
2. Place pear halves on crumbs and sprinkle with lemon juice. Mix brown sugar, salt, cinnamon and nutmeg together. Sprinkle on pears. Add ¼ cup water. Top with remaining crumbs.
3. Bake in a preheated 350° F. oven for 25 minutes. Serve warm with ice cream, if desired.

Makes 6 servings.

Fresh Pineapple Mousse

A luxurious dessert that is almost impossible to make without a processor.

Pulp of 1 large pineapple
  cut to fit Feed Tube
Juice of ½ lemon
3 egg yolks
½ cup sugar
Dash salt

1½ envelopes unflavored gelatin
½ cup cold milk
1 cup heavy cream
2 tablespoons Crème de Menthe
Salad greens

1. Place Disc, shred side up, in Bowl. Process to shred pineapple. Remove to the top of a double boiler. Add lemon juice.
2. Place Blade in Bowl. Add egg yolks, sugar and salt and process to mix. Add this mixture to the pineapple.
3. Sprinkle gelatin in milk and let dissolve 5 minutes. In saucepan, cook pineapple mixture, stirring until mixture coats a metal spoon. Add gelatin and milk and stir. Chill until mixture begins to thicken.
4. Place Beater Accessory in Bowl; whip heavy cream until thick. Add liqueur and fold into pineapple mixture. Fill a 6-cup mold (or the pineapple shell). Refrigerate until firm. To serve, unmold on a bed of greens, or place the filled shell on a platter and surround with greens.

Makes 6 servings.

One of the best desserts you can make with your food processor is fruit ice and sherbet—especially now that the experts are encouraging us to eat lightly. Here are the best of those we tried.

Grapefruit Sherbet

¾ cup sugar
¾ cup water
2 grapefruit, peeled, sectioned and
seeded
½ cup milk

1. In a 2-quart saucepan, bring the sugar and water to a boil over low heat; boil for 2 minutes then allow it to cool.
2. Place Blade in Bowl; add fruit and process until puréed. Add sugar syrup and milk; blend and pour into an ice cube tray; freeze until not quite hard.
3. Remove from freezer and purée again. Repeat this procedure until you have the texture you want.

Makes 6 servings.

Fresh Orange Sherbet

¾ cup sugar
1½ cups water
Rind from ½ of an orange
¼ cup orange juice
1 egg white, beaten to soft peaks
Orange flavored liqueur

1. Boil sugar and water for about 5 minutes; cool.
2. Place Blade in Bowl; process orange rind until finely grated. Add grated rind and orange juice to the syrup; pour into a metal ice tray or shallow baking pan. Freeze until mixture is mushy.
3. Place Blade in Bowl; process mixture until smooth and mix in egg white. Pour back into a tray and return sherbet to the freezer. When it becomes mushy, repeat the process, then return the sherbet to the freezer. About ½ hour before serving move it to the refrigerator section.

Makes 4 servings.

Lime Ice

2 cups water
1 cup freshly squeezed lime juice
   (8 to 10 limes)
1 cup sugar
Rind of 2 limes
2 tablespoons white rum (optional)

1. In a 2-quart saucepan bring water, lime juice and sugar to a boil over low heat. Simmer.
2. Place Blade in Bowl; grate lime rind and add it. Pour into 2 ice trays or a shallow baking pan; freeze until it is almost hard.
3. Remove from freezer, purée and freeze again. Repeat this procedure until you have the texture you want.
4. Just before serving, place Blade in Bowl; add ice and process with white rum, if you wish. Serve in sherbet glasses.

Makes 8 servings.

Raspberry Ice

1 package (10-ounce) frozen
   raspberries
¼ cup sugar
¼ cup orange juice
1 tablespoon lemon juice
Orange-flavored liqueur

1. Place Blade in Bowl. Add all ingredients and purée. Pour the purée in a metal ice cube tray or a shallow baking pan, and place in the freezer until partially frozen.
2. Remove and purée again. Spoon back into the pan and refreeze.
3. Repeat this procedure once or twice more until you have the consistency you desire.
4. About ½ hour before serving, move the tray from the freezer to the refrigerator to allow the ice to soften. Serve in sherbet glasses.

Makes 4 servings.

Fresh Strawberry Ice Cream Cake

**1 pint strawberries, washed and
  hulled**
2 eggs
1 cup sugar
½ cup milk
Juice of 1 lemon
1 cup heavy cream

1. Place Blade in Bowl; purée strawberries. With processor running, add through the Feed Tube, eggs, sugar, milk and lemon juice; blend. Pour into a 9 x 9 x 2-inch metal baking pan and place in freezer until partially frozen.
2. Place Beater Accessory in Bowl; whip cream to soft peaks.
3. Place Blade in Bowl. Empty the strawberry mixture into Bowl and process just to blend with the whipped cream.
4. Pour mixture back into the pan and freeze until firm. Cover with plastic wrap.

Makes 4 servings.

Relishes, Pickles & Preserves

Nothing puts the food processor to better use than the preparation of the foods for canning. Hours of chopping, slicing, mincing, grinding and puréeing can be saved. Stock your kitchen shelves with jars of these and you'll always have something special to serve, or tie a pretty ribbon around a jar of Red Pepper Relish or Peach Chutney for the most welcome of gifts.

Cucumber Relish

4 large cucumbers, unpeeled, cut in
  2-inch pieces
2 large green peppers, cut in 1-inch
  pieces
1 large sweet red pepper, cut in
  1-inch pieces
6 large onions, quartered

6 ribs celery , cut in pieces
¼ cup salt
3½ cups sugar
2 cups white vinegar
1 tablespoon celery seed
1 tablespoon mustard seed

1. Place Blade in Bowl. Chop vegetables, to medium fine, removing to a
   large enamel or stainless steel kettle as Bowl fills up. Sprinkle with salt.
   Cover with cold water. Let stand 4 hours.
2. Drain thoroughly in colander; press out all excess liquid.
3. In the kettle, combine sugar, vinegar, celery seed and mustard seed. Bring
   to a boil, stirring until sugar is dissolved. Stir in drained vegetables,
   simmer 10 minutes.
4. Pack into hot jars to within ½-inch of top. Wipe lids and seal. Process
   in boiling water bath 10 minutes. Cool on racks. Wash and dry jars. Label
   and store in a cool, dark place.

Makes 5 to 6 pints.

Red Pepper Relish

24 red bell peppers,
  cut into quarters
7 medium onions, quartered
2 tablespoons salt

3 cups cider vinegar
3 cups sugar
2 tablespoons mustard seed

1. Place Blade in Bowl. Process to finely chop peppers and onions.
2. Combine in an enamel or stainless steel kettle with salt, vinegar, sugar,
   and mustard seed. Bring to a boil and cook rapidly, uncovered, stirring
   often—about 30 minutes, or until thick.
3. Pack into hot jars, leaving ¼-inch headroom. Wipe rims and seal.
   Process in boiling water bath five minutes. Cool on racks. Label; store
   in a cool, dark place.

Makes 6 pints.

Mustard Pickles

6 (1 to 2-inch long) cucumbers
2 large green peppers, halved and seeded
2 large red peppers, halved and seeded
1 small cauliflower, separated into flowerets
1 pound small white onions
6 green tomatoes, quartered

⅓ cup coarse salt
½ cup packed light brown sugar
3 tablespoons dry mustard
1½ teaspoons turmeric
2 teaspoons mustard seeds
2 teaspoons celery seeds
6 cups cider vinegar
½ cup flour
1 cup cold water

1. Place Disc, slice side up, in Bowl. Slice cucumbers and peppers. Combine with cauliflower, onions and tomatoes in large glass bowl. Sprinkle with coarse salt. Stir to blend well. Cover bowl with plastic wrap and let stand about 12 hours at room temperature.
2. Pour off all liquid and put into a large enamel or stainless steel kettle. Add brown sugar, mustard, turmeric, mustard seeds and celery seeds. Stir in cider vinegar. Bring to a boil, stirring often. Lower heat and simmer 15 minutes. Combine flour and cold water in small bowl and mix to a paste. Stir slowly into bubbling liquid. Cook, stirring constantly, until mixture thickens and bubbles—about 3 minutes.
3. Ladle into hot jars, leaving ½-inch of top. Wipe rims and seal jars. Process in boiling water bath 10 minutes. Cool on racks. Wash and dry jars. Label and store in a cool, dark place.

Makes 8 pints.

Zucchini Pickles

5 pounds zucchini, cut to fit Feed Tube
4 to 5 medium onions, halved
4 cups cider vinegar
2 cups sugar

¼ cup salt
2 teaspoons celery seed
2 teaspoons turmeric
1 teaspoon dry mustard

1. Place Disc, slice side up, in Bowl. Slice zucchini and onions. Remove to a mixing bowl.
2. Combine remaining ingredients in a saucepan. Bring to a boil. Pour over zucchini and onions. Let stand 1 hour, stirring occasionally.
3. Transfer to a large enamel or stainless steel kettle, bring mixture to a boil; simmer 3 minutes. Pour into hot pint jars, leaving ½-inch of top. Be sure vinegar solution covers vegetables. Wipe rims and seal.
4. Process in boiling water bath 15 minutes. Cool, wash jars and dry. Label and store in a cool, dark place.

About 8 pints.

Carrot Almond Conserve

2 pounds carrots, cut in 1-inch
  pieces
4 cups water
2 lemons, quartered

4 cups sugar
½ teaspoon salt
2 cups whole blanched almonds

1. Place Blade in Bowl; process to finely chop carrots. Transfer to an enamel or stainless steel kettle with water, and cook, covered for a few minutes, or until almost tender. Do not drain.
2. Replace Blade in Bowl; finely chop lemons and add to carrots. Add sugar and salt. Cook rapidly for 25 minutes, or until thick, stirring occasionally. Process to finely chop almonds; add to mixture.
3. Pour into hot, sterilized pint jars, leaving ½-inch of top. Wipe rims and seal. Process in boiling water bath 10 minutes. Cool on racks; wash and dry jars; label and store in a cool, dark place.

Makes 6 pints.

Lemon-pear Honey

6 large ripe pears, pared and
  quartered
5 cups sugar

1 lemon, unpeeled, cut to fit
  Feed Tube

1. Place Blade in Bowl. Chop pears fine, and remove to a large saucepan.
2. Place Disc, slice side up, in Bowl. Slice lemon. Add lemon and sugar to pears. Cook and stir until boiling. Reduce heat, cover and simmer until thickened and clear—about 40 to 50 minutes.
3. Ladle into hot sterilized jars, leaving ½-inch of top. Wipe rims and seal. Process in boiling water bath 10 minutes. Cool on racks. Wash and dry jars; label and store in a cool, dark place.

Makes 3 pints.

Peach Chutney

8 peaches, peeled and quartered
1 medium onion, quartered
1 small garlic clove
1 cup raisins
1 cup crystallized ginger

2 tablespoons chili powder
2 tablespoons mustard seed
1 tablespoon salt
1 quart cider vinegar
2¼ cups packed brown sugar

1. Place Blade in Bowl. Process peaches until coarsely chopped. Remove to a large enamel or stainless steel kettle as the Bowl fills. Mince onion, garlic, raisins and ginger. Add to kettle with remaining ingredients. Simmer 1 hour, or until deep brown and thick.
2. Pack into hot jars to within ½-inch of top. Wipe rims and seal jars firmly tight. Place five minutes in a boiling water bath.
3. Remove to rack to cool. Wash and dry jars. Label. Store in a cool, dark place.

Makes 2 to 3 pints.

Pineapple Rhubarb Conserve

½ cup walnuts
6 large stalks rhubarb, cut to fit
    Feed Tube
1 medium orange, sectioned
½ cup raisins
2 sticks cinnamon

2 cups sugar
¾ cup white vinegar
¼ teaspoon cinnamon
⅛ teaspoon ground clove
2 cups fresh, pineapple, in
    1-inch cubes

1. Place Blade in Bowl; pulse to finely chop nuts. Transfer to a small mixing bowl.
2. Place Disc in Bowl; slice rhubarb; empty into a heavy 6-quart pot. Cover rhubarb with boiling water; allow to stand for 3 minutes; drain and return rhubarb to pot.
3. Place Blade in Bowl; process orange and raisins about 15 seconds to finely chop. Add to rhubarb. Add sugar, vinegar, cinnamon and cloves to rhubarb plus pineapple. Stir together. Simmer, stirring occasionally, until thick, about 50 minutes. Stir in nuts.
4. Transfer to a bowl or jar. Will keep several weeks in refrigerator. Serve with poultry, lamb, ham or fish.

Makes 3½ cups.

Index